The Illustrated History of

HEARST CASTLE®

Millionaire publisher William Randolph Hearst and his architect, Julia Morgan, shared a working relationship that began in the very early 1900s and continued for over 40 years of building projects. Their most famous achievement is *La Cuesta Encantada*, Spanish for "The Enchanted Hill," popularly called Hearst Castle. This photograph shows them conferring over construction plans on the estate's Main Terrace. Mr. Hearst and Miss Morgan are facing in the direction of *Casa Grande*, just out of the photo on the right-hand side. (Bison Archives)

On the Front Cover: "Then-and-now" photographs of *Casa Grande*, taken 80 years apart. The complicated construction of Hearst Castle's iconic main building was a lengthy process that began in 1922 and continued for much of the next 25 years. Aside from serving as the residence and business headquarters for William Randolph Hearst, it was also the scene of many memorable social events for celebrities of the era. The art-filled gardens and ornate buildings provided his guests with a Grand Tour of European art and architecture, set against a backdrop of panoramic ocean and mountain views.

The inset photo shows the specialized workers installing the carillon bells into the towers of *Casa Grande* during early 1932. (Archival photo courtesy of Souzan Nelson; color photo by the author)

On the Back Cover: The majestic Neptune Pool was constructed in several phases from 1924 to 1935. *La Cuesta Encantada* was largely hand-built by a generation of dedicated laborers, artisans, designers and landscapers who toiled through the many years of its making. It is now one of California's leading visitor attractions, and Hearst San Simeon State Historical Monument stands as a legacy to their achievements. (Archival photo courtesy of Larry Crawford; color photo by the author)

Half-title Page: (Upper) During a trip to Europe in 1892, 29-year-old William Randolph Hearst sat for this portrait done by his close friend Orrin Peck. It currently hangs in *Casa Grande's* Gothic Study. (Courtesy of Hearst Castle/California State Parks)

(Lower) Aerial view of *La Cuesta Encantada*, Hearst Castle, as it looked soon before opening for tourism in 1958. (Doheny Library, University of Southern California)

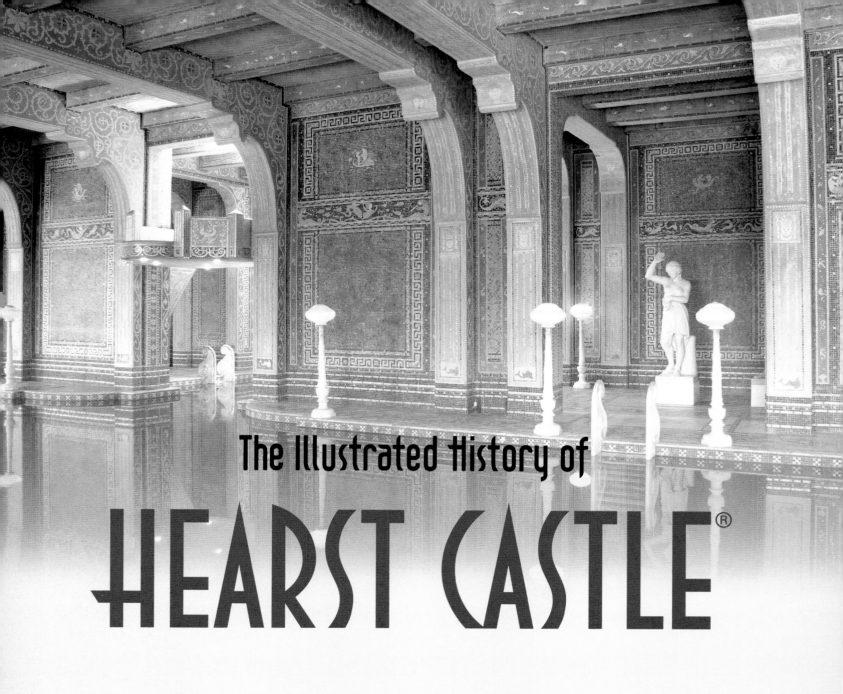

The Illustrated History of

HEARST CASTLE®

Thomas Brown

NOUVEAUX
PRESS

Atascadero, California

To the dedicated and creative builders of La Cuesta Encantada and those who support its legacy, Hearst San Simeon State Historical Monument.

Copyright ® 2012 by Thomas Brown
Second printing, revised and updated 2014
All rights reserved.

ISBN-13: 978-0-615-63927-7
Library of Congress Control Number: 2012912304
Printed in the United States of America
Published by:
Nouveaux Press
9060 Junipero Avenue
Atascadero, California 93422
(805) 462-2206
e-mail: history101@sbcglobal.net

Designed by Inkspot Printing Corp., Lihue, Hawaii
e-mail: print@inkspotkauai.com

CONTENTS

ACKNOWLEDGMENTS

The Illustrated History of Hearst Castle would not have been possible without the extensive help I received from numerous individuals, archives and published works..

I am especially grateful to Hoyt Fields, the Museum Director of Hearst San Simeon State Historical Monument. His immense generosity and assistance made this book possible. Historians Mitch Barrett, Taylor Coffman, Gary Hoving and Robert C. Pavlik all contributed their enormous knowledge to get me started in the right direction and remained my mentors throughout the long process. I endeavor to pay their generosity forward. I was able to do substantial archival research with the generous assistance of: Erin Wighton, Jill Fletcher and Allan Ochs at the San Luis Obispo History Center; Jessica Holada, Peter Runge, Laura Sorvetti, and Catherine Trujillo at the Robert E. Kennedy Library at California Polytechnic University, San Luis Obispo; Susan Snyder at The Bancroft Library, University of California, Berkeley; and Miranda Hambro at the University of California, Berkeley, Environmental Design Archives. All provided me with the use of their excellent facilities and lent invaluable advice and support.

Many archivists and historians provided me with valuable assistance. They include: Erin Chase, Huntington Library; Kristine Krueger, the Margaret Herrick Library at the Academy of Motion Pictures Arts and Sciences; Dace Taube, University of Southern California Doheny Memorial Library; Anne Patterson, Santa Barbara Trust for Historic Preservation; Joan Adan, Forest Lawn Memorial Gardens; Ben Erchul, Caltrans District 5; Dan Calderon and Ray Corbett, Santa Barbara Museum of Natural History; Desiree Lamerdin from the Castlewood Country Club; and Hearst Castle historian Muna Cristal.

Photographic historian-archivists Larry Crawford, Pat Hathaway, and Marc Wanamaker were especially generous in allowing use of photographs from their wonderful collections. It was also my great privilege to be allowed use of family photographs from Kathy Collins, Bill Loorz, Tom Maino, Cy Mamola, Souzan Nelson, Wayne Russell, Marjorie Reid Ramsay-Sewell, and the Hearst Corporation. Their families helped build Hearst Castle and I hope this book is a testimonial to their wondrous achievement.

Writing this book required a thorough foundation of the life of William Randolph Hearst and the immense intricacies that went into the building of Hearst Castle. I benefited greatly from the outstanding works of previous authors, especially: Taylor Coffman, John Dunlap, Geneva Hamilton, Victoria Kastner, Nancy Loe, David Nasaw and Robert C. Pavlik. Many of their books and articles are named in the bibliography at the end of this book. A great blessing was the enthusiastic support I received from Dawn Olsen and John Whitcomb at the Hearst Castle Visitor Center.

A special thanks to my parents, James and Eleanor Brown, who provided an environment conducive to personal growth, and my siblings: Michael Brown, Stephen Brown, Gary Brown, Harold Brown and Valerie Noronha. Lastly, to my wife, Pamela, who immensely helped and encouraged me at every stage, and my "ohana" on the Garden Island of Kauai, especially the creative design work of Josanette Jhoiee Palalay.

Thank you everyone!

Thomas Brown, Atascadero, California

INTRODUCTION

Coastal settlements have historically developed around the calm waters offered by a sheltered bay. The small California community of San Simeon owes its existence to having the only bay along a long stretch of rocky coastline. This area's history of settlement stretches back thousands of years to the Native American peoples, who were in turn largely displaced by 19th-century European colonists who established ranch settlements and mining operations.

In 1863 Joseph Clark established a whaling station at San Simeon Bay. His shore-based hunts of the migrating gray whales were successful enough that he soon added a storage warehouse and several other support buildings. Soon afterwards, in 1865, large portions of local ranch land were bought by George Hearst, a man of great wealth gained in the mining industry. He set about making improvements which included building a shipping pier to service the area's mining, cattle, lumber and seaweed harvesting operations. Although George Hearst's main focus was on the area's commercial possibilities, he also wanted to create a vacation retreat for his wife, Phoebe, and their only child, William Randolph Hearst, who would later become the builder of Hearst Castle.

During the summers of his youth, William Randolph Hearst developed a love for the rural life of San Simeon. The Hearst family frequently camped outdoors and young Will spent many hours exploring the hills on horseback. As an adult he went on to make his own fortune, primarily in the publishing business, beginning with ownership of the *San Francisco Examiner* newspaper. By 1895 he branched out to New York City where he enjoyed great success, and profits, in circulation wars against Joseph Pulitzer's *New York World*.

Although William Randoph Hearst ended up living in New York until well into his middle-age years, he frequently spent summers back at the family ranch. During a visit in 1906 he wrote to his mother: *"I think California is the best country in the world and always will be no matter who comes into it or what is done to it. Nobody or no thing can shut out the beautiful sun or alter the glorious climate."* He signed off with *"Hurrah for dear old California."* Following the death of his parents, he inherited the property and decided it would make an ideal location to build a vacation estate for his wife, children and friends.

The Gilded Age of the late 19th century was an era of magnificent house-mansions built by industrial giants such as Andrew Carnegie and George Vanderbilt. Their great wealth and ability to assemble small armies of craftsmen enabled them to create homes that became landmarks in American architecture. Some were so huge, such as the Biltmore in North Carolina, they included a small town to maintain the needs of the estate. William Randolph Hearst was very knowledgeable about these elaborate homes, and was equally versed in a wide variety of European architecture. He made extensive use of this knowledge during the nearly 30-year period of construction at *La Cuesta Encantada*, the formal name for Hearst Castle, meaning "The Enchanted Hill." The result is one of the most impressive estates built entirely with the wealth of a single individual.

With a beautiful hilltop location, enormous resources and a head filled with ideas, perhaps Hearst's greatest asset was the capable woman who wove it all together. At the very beginning of the process he hired Julia Morgan, a San Francisco architect and graduate of the prestigious Ecole des Beaux-Arts in Paris, France. They shared similar architectural ideas gained from extensive travels in the United States and Europe. Together, they worked through innumerable construction details including how to best utilize Hearst's vast collection of art and antiques. "Miss Morgan," as Hearst respectfully called her, would stay the course through difficulties that she could never have imagined. In the process, she gained the respect of many a hard-nosed construction worker.

Beginning in the mid-1920s, Hearst Castle became a magnet for celebrities of the era. Mr. Hearst's guest list included Hollywood film stars, literary greats, history-making politicians, sports legends and pioneers of aviation. Visitors were invariably amazed by the splendor of the hilltop's elaborately decorated buildings and colorful gardens. They also enjoyed use of the swimming pools, tennis courts and miles of horseback riding trails. There was even a large zoo and animal park.

The Renaissance-themed main house, *Casa Grande*, was the focal point of the evening's activity. A "social hour" was held in the cavernous Assembly Room, the scale of the room's 24-foot-high walls maintained by some equally large antique features: a paneled ceiling of carved walnut, massive stone fireplace and four enormous tapestries portraying Imperial Rome's defeat of the army of Hannibal. Dinner was served in the equally majestic Refectory, where guests' eyes were drawn upward by Gothic arches and colorful heraldic banners. Afterwards, the latest movies (including some produced by Hearst's own studio) were shown in his private theater. Frequently, the actual film stars were in attendance to give impromptu performances under the surreal lighting of the theater's Grecian-style caryatid statues. Guests later retired to bedroom suites that were each uniquely and sumptuously decorated.

Hearst Castle was not only an entertainment mecca; it also became the hub of William Randolph Hearst's media-business empire. The hilltop had a sophisticated telegraph and telephone system that allowed him to maintain constant communication with his newspapers. A short distance away was his private airport and several modern aircraft. Perhaps surprisingly, Hearst was frequently budget-conscious. His plans for *La Cuesta Encantada* were to make it both self-sustaining and profitable. The fruit orchards, livestock, poultry and dairy operations served that purpose and also maintained the ranch's rural heritage.

During the peak years of construction, over 90 workers and household staff were fed and housed on-site. The area was alive with stone carvers, ironwork artisans, restoration specialists, and gardeners; there was even a zookeeper. Ships and trucks arrived at San Simeon loaded with construction materials and furnishings that included Renaissance tapestries, vintage English silver, specially commissioned marble statues, and antiquities from Greece and Rome. The number of items stored in warehouses was so large that some of the packing crates still remained unopened until well after Mr. Hearst's death in 1951.

In many ways, the building of Hearst Castle is the story of the "boom and bust" years of the 1920s and 1930s. It was built by a generation of hard-working artists and tradesmen, many of whom were recent European immigrants. Their dedication and inventiveness are a marvelous success story that continues to awe and inspire new generations of *La Cuesta Encantada* visitors.

(Photo courtesy of Hearst Castle/California State Parks)

THE ORIGINS OF HEARST CASTLE

The mountains of California's Santa Lucia Range parallel the Pacific Ocean from Monterey to San Luis Obispo. Along this rocky coastline, lighthouses built more than a century ago still stand as reminders of the days before radar and global-positioning devices assisted mariners. The hillsides are populated by a wide variety of animals that forage among grassland, oak trees and the remnants of the once-extensive redwood forest. This area is regionally known as the Central Coast, and it has a long history of human habitation that began thousands of years ago with the ancestral Chumash and Salinan Native American hunter-gatherer cultures.

In the year 1542, a small fleet of Spanish ships commanded by Juan Rodriguez Cabrillo sailed along this coastline while searching for the fabled Northwest Passage. At every landfall he claimed ownership for King Charles I of Spain; however, this expedition was unable to find the northern trade route or any great material wealth. Thus, the advent of California's European colonization did not began in earnest until the 1760s, when Spain established several permanent bases and began building a chain of missions that eventually stretched for hundreds of miles. A vital ingredient of their success was to develop self-sustainability by using the local resources to create an economy based primarily on agriculture. During the early years of Spanish rule many large parcels of land were dedicated to livestock ranching, beginning a heritage that has continued through the later transitions of Mexico's independence from Spain, California's 1850 statehood, and into the present day.

Other cultures and ethnic groups contributed towards founding permanent communities along the Central Coast. Among them were Swiss, Portuguese, Chinese, Italian and Japanese immigrants that developed industries in lumber, mining, whaling, dairy and seaweed farming. One of these coastal communities is San Simeon, the home of today's Hearst Castle. The area's heritage of land ownership includes the early Mexican land grants of *Rancho Piedra Blanca*, *Rancho San Simeon* and *Rancho Santa Rosa*.

Beginning in 1865 George Hearst, a wealthy San Francisco resident who made his fortune in mining, began buying major portions of several *ranchos* around San Simeon. His holdings eventually exceeded 66,000 acres and included San Simeon Bay, a very important feature that was being used as a whaling station and port-of-call for ships serving the remote ranching community. By 1878 the area's population and commerce had grown enough for Mr. Hearst to enhance the port facilities by adding a large pier and warehouse. Although his main residence was in bustling San Francisco, George Hearst's roots were rural. At San Simeon he also built a two-story ranch house where he could comfortably vacation with his wife, Phoebe, and their only child, a teenage son named William Randolph Hearst.

During the years of the late 1800s, the Hearst family enjoyed summer picnics atop a prominent hill several miles inland, a location that provided sweeping ocean views and shade from numerous oak trees. Eventually, they erected semi-permanent tents that added a bit of luxury and gave it the quaint name "Camp Hill." William Randolph Hearst's love for the area grew ever stronger over the ensuing years, as he later wrote: *"We had a glorious time there . . . We camped out and fished and rode horseback."* As an adult, "W. R." Hearst would become the 20th century's biggest newspaper and magazine publisher, and among its most interesting personalities. Although much of that time was spent living in New York City, San Simeon's rural life was always close to his heart. Beginning in 1919, he began a nearly 30-year journey of construction that transformed Camp Hill into the magnificent legacy of Hearst Castle.

The Chumash and Salinan Native American people can trace back their ancestry in central California for thousands of years. Though archeological evidence at San Simeon is scarce, this illustration accurately depicts Chumash village life farther to the south. In the year 1793, British explorer Captain George Vancouver wrote in his journals of an encounter with Chumash voyaging canoes off the Central California coast, quite possibly near present-day San Simeon. (Courtesy of the artist, Robert Thomas)

In 1542, Spanish explorer Juan Rodriguez Cabrillo led a small fleet of ships along the uncharted California coastline while searching for riches and northern trade routes. During this quest he claimed much of the land for Spain. The postage stamp on the right honors a later explorer, Gaspar de Portola. During the summer of 1769 his overland expedition passed through present-day San Simeon while heading north to establish a fortified settlement at Monterey. As part of Spain's colonization of California, Franciscan friar Junipero Serra was in San Diego establishing the first of California's 21 missions, a chain that eventually stretched as far north as San Francisco. (Author's collection)

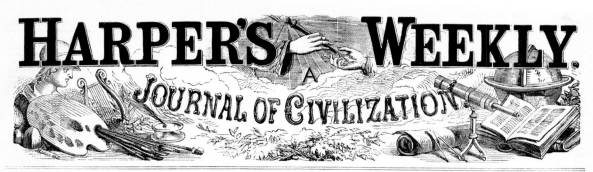

HARPER'S WEEKLY.

JOURNAL OF CIVILIZATION.

Vol. XXI.—No. 1069.]   NEW YORK, SATURDAY, JUNE 23, 1877.   [WITH A SUPPLEMENT. PRICE TEN CENTS.

Entered according to Act of Congress, in the Year 1877, by Harper & Brothers, in the Office of the Librarian of Congress, at Washington.

A WHALING STATION ON THE CALIFORNIA COAST.—Drawn by Frenzeny.—[See Page 483.]

San Simeon Bay's early commercial use was as the supply port for nearby Spanish, and later Mexican, *ranchos* and missions. In the 1860s Joseph Clark established a small base for hunting the migratory gray whales. His crews used longboats to pursue and harpoon the whales and bring them back to shore. This June 23, 1877, issue of *Harper's Weekly* is captioned: "*A Whaling Station on the California Coast.*" It shows the methods that were used to flense the whales and render the blubber to extract the oil.

(Library of Congress)

J.A.J.Wilcox, Boston.

George Hearst

A.L. BANCROFT & CO. PUBLISHERS SAN FRANCISCO.

This engraved portrait is of George Hearst, the father of William Randolph Hearst (the builder of Hearst Castle). George Hearst was born in Franklin County, Missouri, in 1820. As a teenager he became very interested in mining and geology, and gained practical knowledge watching the techniques used at several mines in the area. In 1850 he joined the flow of adventurers looking to find wealth in California's newly discovered gold fields. Although his initial efforts met with little success, he was adept at forming partnerships that bought promising mining operations. In the years ahead, Hearst's ownership in numerous gold, silver and copper mines made him extremely wealthy. Beginning in 1865 he began to invest in agricultural land by buying *ranchos* in the San Simeon area. His purchases included nearly 50,000 acres of *Rancho Piedra Blanca*, the location of today's Hearst Castle.

In George Hearst's senior years he became very active in California's Democratic Party and served for five years as a California Senator before his death in Washington D.C. on February 28, 1891. (History Center of San Luis Obispo)

Phoebe Apperson Hearst was a native of Missouri, born near St. Louis in 1842. She briefly worked as a schoolteacher before her 1862 marriage to George Hearst, who had recently returned following his success in mining. They soon moved to San Francisco where their only child, William Randolph Hearst, was born on April 29, 1863.

During her lifetime, Phoebe Hearst developed a wide range of interests that included travel and world history. When William was 10 years old, she took him on a Grand Tour of Europe that was a cultural immersion that changed their lives. In the years to come, they would each travel extensively and assemble large collections of artwork and antiques from around the world. Phoebe was also a generous contributor to many philanthropic causes, the vast majority relating to education. Perhaps her favorite was the University of California, Berkeley, where she commissioned several important campus buildings and served for 20 years as its first woman regent. Following her death from influenza in 1919, the United States flag was flown at half-mast over many buildings in San Francisco. (Bancroft Library, University of California, Berkeley)

No. 2004. "Mills and Mines." Part of the great Homestake works, Lead City, Dak. Photo and Copyright by Grabill, 1889.

Partial ownership of South Dakota's Homestake Mine was one of the crown jewels of George Hearst's business holdings. The Homestake has been called "America's greatest gold mine" with over 1,375 tons of gold produced until it was shut down in 2002. Another of his investments was the Ophir mine in Nevada's legendary silver-rich Comstock Lode. A commemorative plaque outside nearby Virginia City summarizes George Hearst's mining prowess: *"George Hearst, astute miner, who often bought mines considered valueless and took out rich ore."* (Author's collection)

This 1874 map shows the areas of San Simeon land purchased by George Hearst beginning in 1865. His ownership eventually totaled over 66,000 acres and 14 miles of coastline, encompassing major portions of *Rancho San Simeon, Rancho Santa Rosa* and *Rancho Piedra Blanca* (the future location of Hearst Castle). Hearst bought the land to serve a variety of commercial and personal uses including ranching, raising thoroughbred horses and having a rural alternative to the family's home in San Francisco. (County of San Luis Obispo)

Piedras Blancas light station was completed in 1876 on a small plot of Federal Government land within the cattle grazing land of *Rancho Piedra Blanca*. The light station was established as a response to the many shipwrecks along this rugged stretch of California coastline. It is still in use and can be seen from *La Cuesta Encantada*, the hilltop location of Hearst Castle. The original Fresnel lens seen in this vintage photograph was removed in 1949 and is on display in the nearby town of Cambria. (History Center of San Luis Obispo)

The pier in this 1901 photograph was built by George Hearst to serve the commercial needs of San Simeon's ranches and merchants. Within 20 years, it would be used by ships bringing tons of goods for his son William's construction of Hearst Castle on the hilltop at the far right. A few of these buildings still exist: the warehouse (with the star), Sebastian's Store (just beyond) and the Pacific School (with small tower). Most of the other structures, including the two-story hotels, were torn down in the late 1920s. (History Center of San Luis Obispo)

Many of the ranch workers at San Simeon were experienced *vaqueros* (cowboys) with family ties going back to the earliest days of Spanish and Mexican ownership. The present-day Hearst Ranch still maintains this rural heritage by raising the highest quality open-range beef. (Library of Congress)

Although San Simeon was largely a commercial enterprise, it was used by the Hearst family as a vacation retreat from their city life in San Francisco. In 1878 George Hearst constructed this Italianate style Victorian home about a mile inland from the pier and warehouses. In later years it became known as the Senator's House in deference to George Hearst's later service as a California Senator. Located several miles below Hearst Castle, it is still in use as a private home. (Taylor Coffman)

William Randolph Hearst was molded by the variety of ethnic, rural and metropolitan influences found in 19th century California. As a boy he also had the nickname "Billy Buster" for his prankster-loving nature and love of fireworks . . . a dangerous combination that caused some anxious moments for his parents! Although much of his early youth was spent in San Francisco, the future builder of Hearst Castle would benefit from his many summers at San Simeon. He later reminisced it was where he learned *"to ride after cattle, catch trout or shoot at quail."* Some of that rural background is conveyed in this circa 1870 photo of him taken in San Francisco. (Bancroft Library, University of California, Berkeley)

William Randolph Hearst's career was grounded in newspaper ownership, the first being the *San Francisco Examiner.* He was a journalistic pioneer in making news exciting by using illustrations on the front page and featuring stories that blended hard copy with tabloid-style news. This formula greatly increased his readership and was a huge success when he branched out to New York City in 1895. In the years ahead, Hearst was able to use the "power of the press" to gain enormous popularity and impact local and world politics. (Author's collection)

Newspapers of the era were the public's primary source for information, and became the cornerstone of a Hearst media empire that eventually stretched across the country. He passionately believed that *"A great newspaper is the sword of the people, the shield to protect them from their enemies. It is the banner that leads the march, the lamp which lights the path for popular progress."* (Library of Congress)

Hearst newspapers sometimes used graphic images, similar to this 1898 engraving of the battleship USS *Maine* exploding, to stir public emotions. To say this type of journalism was largely responsible for the resulting Spanish-American War is an oversimplification, although Hearst frequently used his newspapers as a political platform. The explosion of the *Maine* was likely caused by an internal fire which ignited the ship's powder magazine, and not the result of sabotage by Spanish agents. (Library of Congress)

William Randolph Hearst steadily acquired enough newspapers and magazines to effectively reach most households in the country. The *New York American* newspaper and *Good Housekeeping* magazine shown for sale at this New York City newsstand were among the 40 publications in his print media empire when it reached its peak during the mid-1930s. Also noteworthy is the young newsboy, the backbone of newspaper sales for most of the early 20th century.
(Author's collection)

Hearst had a lifelong involvement in American politics and gained enormous popularity by attacking government corruption and advocating improved conditions for the working class. He served in the House of Representatives from 1903 to 1907. His other aspirations to be elected Mayor of New York City, the Governor of New York, and to receive the 1904 Democratic Presidential nomination were unsuccessful. (Author's collection)

On April 18, 1906, San Francisco was struck by a catastrophic earthquake. The resulting fire burned throughout the city for several days, and this period postcard shows the tragic effects to the city's Newspaper Row district. On the left, the gutted structure is the Hearst Building, the home of his *San Francisco Examiner* newspaper. Still on fire is the Call Building, one of the world's first skyscrapers. (Author's collection)

Another view of the devastation on Newspaper Row. The name on the façade identifies the Hearst Building. Mr. Hearst was profoundly affected by the 1906 earthquake and fire, and used many of the resulting advancements in fire protection and structural reinforcement in the later construction at Hearst Castle. (Author's collection)

New York City was where Hearst refined his interest in theater and the new technology of motion pictures. In the late 1890s he met Millicent Willson, a young chorus dancer in the theater district. They were married in 1903 and had five children, all boys, born between 1904 and 1915. The uniforms worn by Millicent and the children in this magazine photo reflect their patriotism during World War I. (Bancroft Library, University of California, Berkeley)

The Clarendon apartment building in New York was the home for publisher Hearst and his family. In 1913, while still a tenant, he sought the landlord's approval for a renovation project that would greatly increase the size of his living quarters. When the request was refused, Hearst instead bought the 12-story building and converted much of it into his business office and luxurious family home. One of the most dramatic additions was this "Great Hall," a Gothic floor where his passion for collecting was displayed by these Medieval tapestries and suits of armor. (Library of Congress)

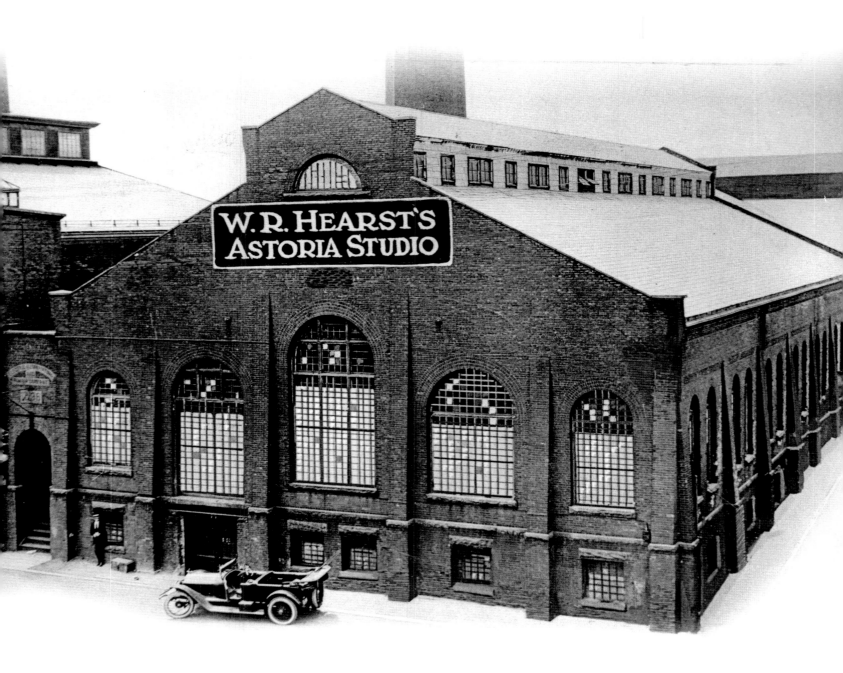

In 1916 William Randolph Hearst ventured into the fledgling movie industry. For much of the next 20 years, he successfully integrated two of his core businesses: the print media and movie-making. His early films of short serials, newsreels and cartoon clips were expanded upon when he branched out into feature-length movie production by forming Cosmopolitan Productions in 1918. After using his newspapers and magazines to present promising stories to the public, Hearst would make the especially popular ones into a movie. This 1921 photograph shows his early studio located in the New York City borough of Queens. At least two movies were made here, *Find the Woman* and *The Beauty Shop,* before operations were moved into a specially constructed studio in Harlem.

In the early 1920s Cosmopolitan Productions moved its operations to Culver City, California, within close proximity to Hollywood. During the landmark years of the 1920s and 1930s, Hearst's partnerships in the film industry included Warner Bros., Paramount Pictures, Metro-Goldwyn-Mayer and Twentieth Centuy-Fox. Some of Cosmopolitan Production's noted accomplishments include transitioning from the silent film era into "talkies" with the enormously popular film *Broadway Melody* in 1929. (Bison Archives)

EARLY YEARS OF CONSTRUCTION
— 1919-1922 —

In April 1919 William Randolph Hearst turned 56 years old. He enjoyed excellent health and a boundless energy which he channeled into politics and the ownership of numerous newspapers, magazines and a movie production company. His mother, Phoebe Apperson Hearst, had recently passed away and left him a wealth of assets in mining stock and real estate, including San Simeon's *Rancho Piedra Blanca*. These enormous resources allowed Hearst to begin the process of fulfilling a long-held ambition: to create a family vacation estate on the same ranch where he experienced rural life as a young boy. The years ahead would bring his dream to fruition with the creation of *La Cuesta Encantada,* the formal name for Hearst Castle, meaning "The Enchanted Hill."

With experience gained from numerous trips to Europe, Hearst preferred the Gothic, Renaissance and Moorish architectural styles of southern Spain, Italy and North Africa. He was also influenced by Spanish Colonial Revival, a California style made popular following its use at the 1915 Panama Canal exhibitions held in San Diego and San Francisco. In May 1919 Hearst met with his architect, Julia Morgan, in her San Francisco office to discuss building at San Simeon. Their next meeting, in August, would be at "Camp Hill" to evaluate the precise building site that would best incorporate the ocean and mountain views. Other discussions included suitability of a nearby rock quarry for concrete production and obtaining hydroelectric power from the natural springs in the area. In the weeks ahead, Morgan submitted a variety of design studies to Hearst. From these, a blend of architectural styles was developed that can be broadly described as Southern Mediterranean Renaissance. Contributing to the variety of architecture eventually used at Hearst Castle was the need to incorporate a wide diversity of elements from Hearst's antique collection. These ranged from ancient Roman temple fragments to medieval iron gates. Interior spaces were sometimes designed around enormous Renaissance ceilings, tapestries and stone fireplace mantels. Hearst and Morgan were perfectionists and the process was fraught with experimentation and innovation. Construction workers at the site were constantly challenged by the hardships of living and working at such a remote location. Some embraced the process and stayed for many years while others couldn't pack their bags quickly enough.

The design called for a group of three houses, each with a unique design and view, arranged in a semi-circle around a large and elaborate main house. This main building, named *Casa Grande,* would feature twin bell towers and be the planned residence for Mr. and Mrs. Hearst. A separate landscape design called for the entire group of buildings to be linked by terraces, walkways and a meandering garden feature called the Esplanade. Additional plans later followed that expanded the existing *Rancho Piedra Blanca* cattle ranch with dairy, poultry and agricultural operations. Fortunately, there was already a commercial pier and warehouse at nearby San Simeon Bay to accommodate the huge volume of construction materials needed for the project. The first shipment of supplies to leave San Francisco Bay was described by Julia Morgan in a letter to Hearst, written on November 21, 1919: *"The 'Cleone', a very disreputable old coaster, sailed yesterday from the Oakland side for San Simeon, fully insured, with cement, lumber for forms, nails, reinforcing bars for concrete, ready roofing and a second-hand band saw and rock crusher. It should reach your wharf Sunday."*

William Randolph Hearst initially pushed for a summer 1920 completion. Given the immense scope of *Casa Grande* alone, this soon proved to be an impossible time frame. However, the construction blueprints for the three smaller houses were advanced enough for their groundbreaking to begin in February 1920. Each house was eventually given an individual name: *Casa del Monte* (House of the Mountain, for its view of the Santa Lucia coastal range), *Casa del Sol* (House of the Sun, for having dramatic sunset views) and the largest, *Casa del Mar* (House of the Sea, for its expansive coastline views).

Soon after construction began, the building site revealed its many challenges: strong winter storms, bad roads, supply problems and a rapid turnover of workers. These problems were also compounded by Hearst's frequent changes that added to the scope of

Chapter 2

EARLY YEARS OF CONSTRUCTION
— 1919-1922 —

the project. The resulting delays ensured the family's 1920 summer visit from New York would again require the use of camping tents. Throughout these difficulties, and for many years to come, William Randolph Hearst benefited from a cadre of loyal employees who specialized in fabricating from wood, metal and cast stone. It is certainly remarkable that the construction site was largely controlled by Julia Morgan, who may have been small in stature but was a powerful and respected presence.

During the first half of 1921, work focused on completing the interiors of the houses. Two of them, *Casa del Sol* and *Casa del Monte,* were rushed to a temporary state of completion for the Hearst's upcoming summer visit. With the first phase of hilltop construction nearly finished, Hearst and Morgan once again focused their attention on building *Casa Grande.* Groundbreaking for its foundation began in the late spring of 1922; the concrete pouring for this enormous structure would require a large mobilization of workers and be the biggest project undertaken thus far.

Upon the death of his mother, Phoebe, in early 1919, William Randolph Hearst inherited a wealth of mining stock, cash and real estate. Included was a huge parcel of ranch land along California's central coast, a portion of which is shown in this 1930s photograph. In the upper left corner is *La Cuesta Encantada*, commonly known today as Hearst Castle. Many of the supplies used for its construction were brought to San Simeon Bay by small ships, such as the one tied up at the pier. At the time of this photo, the current Highway 1 coastal road was still several years away from completion. (Loorz Family Collection)

The Hearst family's early name for *La Cuesta Encantada* was Camp Hill, given during their many summer camping trips. William Randolph Hearst was equally comfortable enjoying the ranch life or running his many businesses from his New York and California offices. However, he was 56 years old upon inheriting the San Simeon property and expressed, *"I get tired going up there and camping in tents. I'm getting a little old for that."* This laid the groundwork for his decision in 1919 to construct what would become Hearst Castle. (Bancroft Library, University of California, Berkeley)

Among the properties inherited by "W.R." Hearst was this ranch estate outside Pleasanton, California. Named *Hacienda del Pozo de Verona*, after a Renaissance-era Italian wellhead that decorated the front courtyard, it had been one of his mother's favorite homes. Its pastoral location, gardens, and guest amenities inspired many of W.R.'s decisions in the making of Hearst Castle. Also, the use of the *Hacienda's* blend of Mission Revival and Pueblo adobe architectural styles was briefly considered during the early design discussions. Another parallel between both estates is the key role played in their construction by San Francisco architect Julia Morgan.

During the mid-1920s, Hearst sold the property and an 18-hole golf course was added. Renamed Castlewood Country Club, most of the original *Hacienda* structures seen in this photograph were destroyed by fire in 1969. (Courtesy of Larry Crawford)

Hearst firmly believed that architecture was an art form unto itself. San Francisco's 1915 Panama-Pacific International Exposition was held to commemorate the United States completion of the Panama Canal, and showcased the city's recovery from the 1906 earthquake. He was actively involved in the fair's organization and paid close attention to the architectural designs created by the fair's architects. The Spanish, Moorish and Venetian styles shown in this photograph have direct parallels in the designs that were used in the building of Hearst Castle. (Author's collection)

A second 1915 world's fair, the Panama-California Exposition, was hosted in San Diego. Julia Morgan, Hearst's architect for nearly all the construction at Hearst Castle, was very familiar with the wide variety of architecture that was used in both venues. The San Diego fair's frequent use of Spanish Colonial Revival, as seen in this advertisement, brought the style into vogue. It would become among the early favorites for Hearst Castle's architectural theme. In the end, the variety of its construction reflects a composite of many stylistic influences that perhaps can be broadly described as Southern Mediterranean Renaissance.
(Author's collection)

Perhaps the most recognizable feature at Hearst Castle is *Casa Grande*, the iconic main building with twin bell towers. Much of its inspiration was drawn from *Santa Maria la Mayor*, a 16th-century Catholic church in Ronda, southern Spain. Julia Morgan's early design studies were traced directly from a photograph (very similar to this postcard) found in a book published in 1917: *The Minor Ecclesiastical, Domestic and Garden Architecture of Southern Spain*. It is quite possible that Mr. Hearst visited the church during one of his trips to Europe. Appropriate to the variety of architectural themes used at Hearst Castle, its construction is a composite of Renaissance and Gothic architecture. (Author's collection)

From these humble beginnings Hearst Castle arose. Tents were used by the Hearst family during summer camping trips, and also by the workers in the early years of construction. The meagre amenities, and remote location, made it very difficult to maintain an adequate work force. Hearst biographer Mrs. Fremont Older wrote: *"The men lived in tents and used oil lamps. At night, large fat tarantulas sometimes shot out of the bedding. Daytime was rendered interesting by hissing rattlesnakes."* Ranch buildings and San Simeon Bay can be seen in the far distance. (Courtesy of the Hearst Corporation)

During the early years of construction nearly all supplies arrived from San Francisco via small coastal freighters. The reverse of this photograph is captioned: "Steamer *Admiral Nicholson* leaving San Simeon wharf." Regular runs brought cargoes of cement, rebar and lumber. Supplies were then loaded onto trucks for the five-mile journey to the hilltop work site. (History Center of San Luis Obispo)

The construction schedule initially called for a June 1920 completion of *Casa Grande,* the immense main building and proposed future residence for Mr. and Mrs. Hearst. It was an overly ambitious plan and quickly shelved. The spring and summer of 1920 were instead spent on pouring the foundations and walls of the three smaller houses. Each house was given a Spanish name inspired by their view orientation; here framing has begun on the second floor of *Casa del Monte* (House of the Mountain). (Courtesy of the Hearst Corporation)

All construction at Hearst Castle required extensive use of steel-reinforced concrete, a lesson learned from the devastating 1906 San Francisco earthquake. This view of *Casa del Monte* also shows the site of the future Neptune Pool in the flat area between the groves of oak trees. (Courtesy of the Hearst Corporation)

Between 1919 and 1937 more than 90 shipments of antique furnishings were sent by rail to California from William Randolph Hearst's warehouses in New York. He described one of these shipments in a letter to Julia Morgan: *"I have sent various other marbles and terra cottas for external decoration . . . also many gold and polychrome wood columns and door frames."* This procession of trucks leaving the San Luis Obispo train station (the nearest one to San Simeon) is bringing furnishings for the houses being built atop *La Cuesta Encantada*. Much of the arduous 45-mile journey was over unpaved roads. (Hearst Castle/California State Parks)

Julia Morgan received her architectural degree as the first female graduate of the prestigious Ecole de Beaux-Arts in Paris, France. She and Mr. Hearst are shown here conferring in *Casa del Monte's* courtyard during the fall of 1920. Of their working relationship, she later recalled: *"Mr. Hearst and I are fellow architects. He supplies the vision and critical judgment. I give technical knowledge and building experience."* Hearst would sometimes jokingly sign his letters *"Viollet-de-Luc Hearst"* (a reference to the famous 19th-century French Gothic Revival architect). (Hearst Castle/California State Parks)

By mid-1921 two of the houses, *Casa del Monte* (House of the Mountain) and *Casa del Sol* (House of the Sun), were complete enough to allow the Hearst family to dispense with using the camping tents. The packing crates in this view of *Casa del Monte* show the rushed nature of final preparations for their arrival from New York. Note the building's ornamentation; attention to detail was a signature aspect for all the hilltop architecture. The gentleman in the foreground is likely California Senator James D. Phelan. (California Views)

William Randolph Hearst and Millicent Hearst on the Esplanade walkway outside the newly completed *Casa del Monte,* July 1921. During their visits over the next several years, the Hearsts would use this house while awaiting the completion of the larger, and more sumptuous, *Casa del Mar.* Mrs. Hearst provided extensive input in the early years of construction; she had even christened the hilltop *Las Estrellas* (The Stars). It was soon discovered that this romantic name was already being used at a neighboring ranch, and a new name was chosen—*La Cuesta Encantada* (The Enchanted Hill). (California Views)

One reason for the lengthy building process was the elaborate interior construction of each house. European antiques were used for much of the furnishings and the built-in features included large intricate ceilings of plaster of Paris. This *Casa del Mar* (House of the Sea) bedroom shows that Hearst frequently put aside his budgetary concerns for extravagant artistic effects. The interior of this house was so complex that it wasn't finished until 1924. (Hearst Castle/California State Parks)

In a letter dated September 1922, Hearst wrote to Julia Morgan: *"Mrs. Hearst says the driving of automobiles around the terrace road is going to spoil the big inner court as a living court . . . I believe she is exactly right."* This photo dates from that time, and is one of the few that shows vehicle use on the Esplanade. The transition to a garden walkway created one of *La Cuesta Encantada's* most endearing features. (Family of Mary Moro Villa)

Everything used to construct Hearst Castle was trucked five miles up the steep and unpaved road. Not an easy task, as seen with this truck that has slipped off the shoulder. Palm trees were one of the earliest major landscape features used at Hearst Castle and most are still thriving . . . and have grown significantly taller! (History Center of San Luis Obispo)

La Cuesta Encantada in the summer of 1922. Within three years this view would be greatly changed by acres of landscaping, orchards and the grand edifice of *Casa Grande* crowning the hilltop. (Doheny Library, University of Southern California)

This photo originally appeared in the memoirs of Charles A. Maino, a local supplier of Hearst's trucks and automobiles. He described his first encounter with the eccentric millionaire: *"A large man in rumpled shabby clothes came into the garage to order a truck for his ranch. As the sale progressed, the stranger added more and more extras that added a considerable amount to the base price. When asked how much he would put down on the sale, the man took out a checkbook and said, 'I will pay for it now.' He wrote out the entire amount and signed the check William Randolph Hearst."* (Courtesy of the V. J. Maino family)

The landscape architecture plan called for all the houses to be connected by a series of terraces and walkways. This is the first version of the West Terrace, located just below *Casa del Sol*. Beyond the wall are newly planted juvenile citrus trees. Within several years, acres of fruit orchards would cover the nearby hills. (History Center of San Luis Obispo)

Freshwater springs located several miles from the hilltop provided the water source for orchard irrigation, concrete mixing and hydroelectric power (the electrical source until public utility service began in the mid-1920s). Above-ground pipes connect to this 100,000 gallon reservoir that was built in 1922. The same springs continue to supply much of the water needs of Hearst Castle and the adjoining ranch. (Hearst Castle/California State Parks)

The first reservoir wasn't sufficient for the expanding needs of Mr. Hearst's estate. This view shows construction of the much larger one, holding 1.5 million gallons, that was added in the late 1920s. His attention to detail can be appreciated by the decision to plant a small forest of conifer trees to hide both reservoirs from view at nearby *La Cuesta Encantada*. Everything appears quiet on the day this photo was taken, except for the fancy automobile that probably belonged to the photographer. (Hearst Castle/ California State Parks)

Hearst Castle's grounds abound with sculptures and other decorative stone artworks. Some are of ancient origin while others are 20th century copies, such as *Crouching Venus,* purchased by Hearst in 1920 for $275. This photograph shows Venus in her original location in the lily pond behind *Casa del Monte.* In 1929 this pond was covered over by the expansive North Terrace and the sculpture moved to the house's courtyard. (Bison Archives)

A major feature on the hilltop is the Main Terrace's lily pond, the home for Leopoldo Ansiglioni's sculpture *Galatea on a Dolphin.* This sculpture is one of several examples he carved in the 1880s, and was much admired by William Randolph Hearst while on a trip to Italy in 1889. Lacking the necessary funds, he instead convinced his mother to buy it for her own art collection. In the early 1920s, *Galatea* became one of the first landscape decorations used at Hearst Castle. The original lily pond basin, seen in this early 1920s photograph, was greatly enlarged several years later. (History Center of San Luis Obispo)

By mid-1922 work was ready to begin on the construction of *Casa Grande*, the main building and projected residence for Mr. and Mrs. Hearst. This elevation drawing from the San Francisco office of Julia Morgan has a notation that the precise location was established by Mr. Hearst in a telegram dated December, 1921. The entire hilltop had been surveyed several years earlier to determine the optimal scenic views, and such preliminary sketches also showed the visual effect the buildings would have on each other.

Casa Grande is clearly the focal point, and faces towards the Pacific Ocean five miles away and 1,600 feet below. It overlooks the three "guest houses" and the native oak tree landscaping of the central plaza and surrounding terraces. (Hearst Castle/California State Parks)

This whimsical photo shows the playful side of William Randolph Hearst. He had an amazing ability to manage a complex business and personal life while also being fully involved in his building projects. (Bancroft Library, University of California, Berkeley)

Excavation work on the foundation for *Casa Grande* began in June, 1922, heralding a project that would crown the hilltop with the iconic feature that eventually comprised four stories and 115 rooms. This photograph gives an idea of the scale of the concrete work needed to top the first floor. The large metal tower (called the hoisting tower) was used to lift batches of concrete that were then poured down a sluice to make the 24-foot-high interior walls. (Hearst Castle/California State Parks)

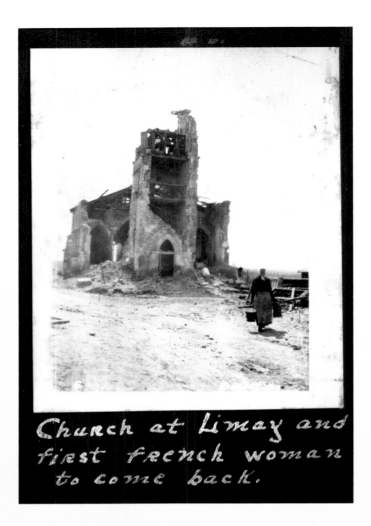

Church at Limay and first french woman to come back.

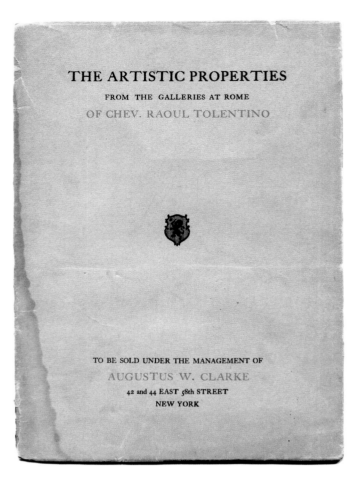

THE ARTISTIC PROPERTIES

FROM THE GALLERIES AT ROME

OF CHEV. RAOUL TOLENTINO

TO BE SOLD UNDER THE MANAGEMENT OF

AUGUSTUS W. CLARKE

42 and 44 EAST 58th STREET
NEW YORK

World War 1 had a devastating effect on Europe's economy. By the early 1920s, many European institutions and family estates were raising money by selling their art treasures and historical items. Mr. Hearst regularly purchased antiques through international art dealers and by perusing the offerings found in the catalogs of auction houses (especially from New York, as in this example from November 1922). His preference was the Gothic and Renaissance eras, with a particular eye towards finding furnishings for the huge rooms of *Casa Grande*: tapestries, carved stone fireplaces and window frames, sculptures, paintings, and rows of elaborately carved choir stalls to provide scale for the tall interior walls. The full-time staffs at Hearst's several warehouses were challenged in keeping up with the incoming flow, and Julia Morgan was kept equally busy deciphering how to best use everything within the constraints of design and construction.

The bottom photograph, taken in the mid-1920s, shows a variety of these items being used in the furnishing of *Casa Grande's* Assembly Room. The bronze sculpture is German artist Victor Seifert's *"Trinkender Frauenakt"* (Drinking Nymph).

(Upper photos, author's collection; lower, History Center of San Luis Obispo)

Chapter 3

A CASTLE IN THE CLOUDS EMERGES
— 1923-1925 —

William Randolph Hearst did not visit *La Cuesta Encantada* from June 1922 through mid-1923. He spent most of that time in New York City, his primary residence and business headquarters. However, construction remained brisk at his vacation estate where Julia Morgan oversaw nearly every aspect while acting as his architect, project supervisor, interior designer and landscape artist. Together, they sorted out the details of architecture and horticulture through a steady stream of letters and telegrams. In much of this correspondence Hearst discussed specific antique fixtures he had bought, or was considering to buy, and frequently left it to "Miss Morgan" to decide how to best use them.

Another of Julia Morgan's responsibilities was maintaining the construction account. Its financial balance ebbed and flowed depending on Mr. Hearst's many other business and personal expenses. The occasional lack of funds would frequently have Hearst ordering an imminent layoff of the workforce, only to be quickly countermanded by his infusion of fresh money and new projects. The number of staff employed at *La Cuesta Encantada* usually ranged from 30 to 90, with as many as 125 if multiple large projects were happening simultaneously. By the early 1920s, much of the hilltop had evolved into a nearly self-sufficient construction community.

The main focus of construction during this period was the completion of *Casa Grande*. The amount of concrete needed to pour the façade took several months during 1923 and was called "The Big Pour." Construction continued at a rapid pace on the building's towers, which were capped off by early 1924. These first-style towers, sometimes called pinnacles by Hearst, had slender pointed tops and did not contain bells. Within the ground floor Assembly Room and Refectory, their Renaissance and Gothic treatments were achieved by the installation of 15th- and 16th-century antique wood ceilings, stone entryways and fireplace mantels. Their interiors also included a large number of choir stalls, used as decorative wainscoting, and enormous Flemish tapestries from Hearst's vast collection. Everything was seamlessly integrated by specialized artisans using the hilltop's cast stone, woodworking and wrought-iron workshops.

The initial construction and landscaping of the Esplanade and terraces was also largely complete by 1924. The guest houses were finished and their courtyards and exteriors each had a different floral theme, providing the colorful look that is still seen today. There were acres of citrus and conifer saplings, many grown in the hilltop nursery, planted on the hills outside the perimeter walls.

Hearst had long wanted a swimming pool on the hilltop, and a relatively modest one was rushed to completion in time for use during the family's visit in the summer of 1924. It was soon called the Neptune Pool because of the Roman god Neptune statuary group that was used as a landscaping feature. Beginning in 1925, the pool was completely rebuilt into a much larger and elaborate version. In the years ahead even grander plans would transform it into one of Hearst Castle's most recognizable features.

By the summer of 1925, *La Cuesta Encantada* was taking on a finished appearance. Mr. and Mrs. Hearst had already hosted many guests, including friends and associates from the Hollywood movie industry. Perhaps these early visitors shared the impression of one of their contemporaries, Oscar-winning designer Sir Cecil Beaton, who later wrote: *"It was right out of a fairy story . . . a vast sparkling white castle in Spain."* It may have seemed like a fantasy on the outside, but undercurrents of change within the Hearst marriage would soon usher in a new era at *La Cuesta Encantada*.

Hearst was frequently called "W. R." by his friends and "The Chief" by his many business associates. This photograph shows him on the steep hillside below *Casa del Mar* (on the right) in July, 1923. During that summer's visit, he and Millicent were able to use this largest, and most extravagant, of the guest houses for the first time. Work was still underway inside, including the year-long process of gilding and painting the cast-plaster Hero ceiling for one of the bedrooms.

During the early years of construction, serious consideration was given to creating a total of five guest houses, all arranged in a semi-circle along the Esplanade. However, progress on the final two never went beyond the planning stage and some preliminary concrete work. (Author's collection)

LA CUESTA ENCANTADA

CASA DEL MAR

LA CUESTA ENCANTADA

CASA DEL SOL

LA CUESTA ENCANTADA

CASA DEL MONTE

Engraved stationery was printed for each of the three guest houses. In the years ahead, it would be used by many famous guests writing of their enjoyable stay in the luxurious accommodations found at "Mr. Hearst's Ranch."
(History Center of San Luis Obispo)

Pouring concrete for the main floors and towers of *Casa Grande* took all of 1923 and into 1924. This photograph was taken during the several-months-long "Big Pour" period, when the building's façade and lower towers were created. It is worth noting that overhead cranes were not used in the making of Hearst Castle's buildings and pools; most of the major concrete work was done using the tall "hoisting tower" seen here, along with a system of pulleys, sluices and hand labor.

Details seen on the left-hand side include framing of the lower terrace walls below *Casa del Monte*, and the wood buildings and water tower of the early construction camp. On the right is *Casa del Sol*. (Cal Poly, San Luis Obispo)

The inscription on this photo reads: *"Concrete truss in Main Building 12/20/23."* Much of California is earthquake prone and the construction of *Casa Grande* called for extensive use of reinforced concrete. Walter Huber was the structural engineer for this specialty work. (Hearst Castle/California State Parks)

Concrete is a mixture of aggregate, sand and cement. The process is shown in the foreground, and the batch was then loaded into a hopper and hoisted up the tall metal tower for pouring into the forms. This view shows *Casa Grande's* southern and east-facing sides. On the left, framing of the southern bell tower is nearly complete. The eastern side of the building faces the Santa Lucia Range, and it was greatly modified in the years ahead to create the elaborate Doge's Suite and Duplex bedrooms. Note the construction worker standing atop the hoisting tower. (Hearst Castle/California State Parks)

The mild winter of 1923-24 allowed significant headway to be made on pouring the concrete of *Casa Grande's* façade and towers. Julia Morgan described the progress in a letter to Hearst back in New York: *"Mr. Rossi [the construction superintendent] is on the 'big pour' which fills up to and over the roof before it halts. I never saw men working so very hard with so much smiling good will as that polyglot crew of his."* (Hearst Castle/California State Parks)

Pouring *Casa Grande's* exterior shell and towers was completed in March 1924. Following the removal of the concrete forms and framework, the roof was made watertight and the building's elaborate interior construction began. These early towers were called "pinnacles" by Hearst, and contain large water tanks made from non-corrosive Monel metal on the level above the arched openings. (Hearst Castle/California State Parks)

The open space within the arched windows was originally designed for the electrically playable carillon bells, an idea that was temporarily shelved when Mrs. Hearst decided *Casa Grande* was beginning to look "too church-like." During the early to mid-1930s, this upper-floor area within each tower was used to create the beautifully decorated Celestial bedrooms. (Bancroft Library, University of California, Berkeley)

Julia Morgan was unbothered by heights, as can be seen from this letter written to Hearst following one of her inspection trips: *"Yesterday I had a pleasant walk along the completed ridge pole of the main building roof. The view is 'GREAT' and the lovely clear weather allowed one to see way up and down the coast."* Her view from atop newly poured *Casa Grande* would have been similar to this panorama taken in mid-1924, showing the Esplanade and (left to right): *Casa del Mar, Casa del Sol* and *Casa del Monte*. (History Center of San Luis Obispo)

One of the main components of Hearst and Morgan's design was a comprehensive plan for landscape architecture. A largely neoclassical effect was created, as seen in this circa 1924 photograph taken along the Esplanade (note *Casa Grande* on the right). The sculpture is a 19th-century rendition of Italian sculptor Antonio Canova's *The Three Graces*. The sarcophagus demonstrates the complexities that "W.R." Hearst faced when collecting antiquities. He purchased it as being authentic 1st-century Roman; however, it is now thought likely to be a clever forgery. (History Center of San Luis Obispo)

The large number of artworks arriving for display on the hilltop included German sculptor Fritz Behn's rendition of the mythological Greek goddess *Europa*. As can be seen, rollers were used to move the heavy marble statue to its permanent location in one of the Esplanade's floral gardens. In the background, scaffolding still encloses the north side of *Casa Grande*. (Hearst Castle/California State Parks)

After more than four years of construction, many of *La Cuesta Encantada's* major features can be seen in this aerial photograph taken in the summer of 1924 (although another decade of construction would alter many of them). Inside the recently poured concrete shell of *Casa Grande*, the immense task of furnishing its interior spaces has begun. An outdoor pool was being added to the garden area behind the oak trees in the center foreground. The large tent, on the left, was used as a warehouse and construction headquarters. It was also where movies were shown until the location was taken over by construction of the first tennis court the following year. (Detail - Cal Poly, San Luis Obispo)

Water features had long been a part of the hilltop's landscaping plans. A major project for 1924 was building a "plunge" (an archaic name for swimming pool) in time for the Hearst family's annual summer visit from New York. These two photographs show the construction and completion of the earliest version of the Neptune Pool. Within the partially uncrated boxes is its namesake: three sculptures collectively called *Neptune and the Nereids*.
(History Center of San Luis Obispo)

The uncompleted concrete feature in the foreground is the "cascades," a stepped series of water basins that was crowned at the top by *Neptune and the Nereids.*

The Neptune Pool experienced nearly constant modifications during the years from 1924 to 1935, and this first version survived for less than two years before construction began on a much larger replacement.
(Cal Poly, San Luis Obispo)

The sculpture group *Neptune and the Nereids* has a long history at the Neptune Pool. Hearst's first recorded interest in its purchase was back in 1922 when he wrote Julia Morgan of the *"dominant figure of an elderly gentleman with whiskers who lends respectability to the landscape— for those at least who don't know his record . . . I think I will get him. We can use him <u>somewhere.</u>"* Hearst's reference to "his record" likely refers to the extensive virile conquests of the Greek and Roman gods Poseidon and Neptune. (History Center of San Luis Obispo)

This caption is on the reverse of a *Neptune and the Nereids* photo originally kept in Hearst's inventory records. The sculpture's Italian origins are traced from the 17th century Doria Palace to 19th century composer Giuseppe Verdi (whose renowned operas include *Aida* and *Rigoletto*). It also shows its purchase by Hearst from "P. W. French & Co.," one of New York City's preeminent art dealers. The sculpture group was shipped in 1923 to San Simeon and soon given a prominent place overlooking the Neptune Pool. It eventually became the crowning feature in the 1935 construction of the pool's Roman temple.
(Environmental Design Archives, University of California at Berkeley)

P.C. No. 5683   Photo #565?

An 17th Century Italian Fountain
"Neptune and Nereids"
white marble - Stone
from Doria Palace
and Maestro Verdi Collection

Price $12000.—
Crates 1458-1463 inc – 19th Cen
Shipped San Simeon July 17, 1923

P. W. French & Co

July 1921

At the center, Neptune stands with trident in left hand; below are two undraped female figures reclining on sea animals.

While the exterior work of *Casa Grande* was in progress, master wood carver Jules Suppo had been creating the building's cornice and pediment at his San Francisco studio. The fanciful theme of animals and heraldic symbols came from *Arte y Decoración en España,* a book published in 1918 that contains photographs of very similar carvings found on a house in Sanguesa, northern Spain. (Hearst Castle/California State Parks)

La Cuesta Encantada shows its extensive progress in late 1925. Camille Rossi was the construction superintendent during this period and had the enormously difficult job of taking Julia Morgan's blueprints and making them a tangible reality. The hoisting tower, recently used to pour the concrete for *Casa Grande,* is being re-erected near the central grove of oak trees to create a major enlargement of the Neptune Pool. Acres of citrus orchards were planted on the slopes below the terrace walls to augment the ranch's existing cattle operations. (History Center of San Luis Obispo)

A detail of *Casa Grande's* cornice ornamentation. Full-sized plaster models were made in the hilltop casting workshops for Jules Suppo to replicate at his San Francisco studio. He carved everything from large blocks of Siamese teakwood, which were then transported in sections for installation. The process extended over two years, from 1923 to 1924. (Author's contemporary photograph)

43

During the peak periods of construction, from the mid-1920s to the mid-1930s, up to 90 workers were housed in the hill-top's permanent work camp. This photograph shows the "Hearst Camp" mess hall, where the kitchen staff served the men three hearty meals, seven days a week. Surviving menus give an idea of a typical dinner: steak, fried potatoes, spaghetti, string beans, olives, cherries, cake, bread, coffee and tea. (Loorz Family Collection)

Sebastian Bros. was the nearest source for purchasing general goods. The grandson of Hearst's orchardist Nigel Keep aptly described the small parcel of land it was built upon: *"Sebastian's store was private property in this expanse of Hearst-owned land."* The store's rich history dates back to the early whaling days and is a historical landmark still in operation. It still looks much the same as in this photograph dating from Hearst Castle's early years. (Loorz Family Collection)

The surrounding hills and natural springs were home to bobcats, deer, bears, coyotes, quail and fish. Although Hearst would occasionally offer a bounty on wildlife that were dangerous to his livestock or zoo animals, he would not otherwise allow his workers hunting or fishing privileges. (History Center of San Luis Obispo)

William Randolph Hearst's concept for *La Cuesta Encantada* was twofold: a working ranch and vacation estate for his family and friends. One of the ways he fulfilled this dual purpose was by establishing an animal park alongside the private road that led to the hilltop. Some of his many game animals included camels, zebras, ostriches, llamas and antelope. (Hearst Castle/California State Parks)

Herds of buffalo and other large grazing animals roamed the lower slopes of the ranch property. Employees, and guests arriving by automobile, were cautioned that animals had the right-of-way; a practice that irritated the workers that were continually running truckloads of supplies up the hill. Even today, descendants of these zebras can occasionally be seen along the coastal highway near San Simeon. (Ullstein Bild)

Ranch operations included livestock, dairy and poultry. Adela Rogers St. Johns, a famous writer during this era and frequent visitor to Hearst Castle, recalled: *"We all called it the Ranch, or Hearst Ranch. This was not phony at all, it was the real thing. He ran it as a ranch, with cattle in every direction."* The beef cattle roamed on open range, so this load of hay may be destined for the stables. Numerous horses were used by the cowboys who tended the cattle herds, and up to 40 were kept at the hilltop stable for guests to use on trail rides. (Marjorie Reid Ramsay-Sewell)

In addition to animals grazing on the lower slopes, by the mid-1920s a separate zoo had been established on the hilltop a short distance from *Casa Grande*. In the years ahead, it would grow enormously to include dozens of exotic animals including lions, tigers and bears. This young musician is likely one of the employees that worked in the camp kitchen. (Loorz family collection)

Hearst, on the left, loved to lead his guests on picnics into the surrounding hills. Riding on horseback was frequently the mode of transport, with an advance party of kitchen staff sent via truck and automobiles to prepare what has been described as a "baronial feast" of potatoes and barbequed beef. For those guests too saddle-sore to continue, the automobiles were a welcome sight! (Loorz family collection)

Mr. Hearst was an adept tennis player and the sport was a popular activity on the hilltop. This rare photograph shows the first tennis court, which was built behind *Casa Grande* in the summer of 1925. A second court was added in 1927, but this view soon changed when construction began on the building that houses the indoor Roman Pool and two rooftop tennis courts.

The blue pencil sketch on the north tower of *Casa Grande* is original to the photo, and shows that planning had already begun for enlarging the towers. Modern-day visitors to Hearst Castle board their departure buses from the same spot as the automobile seen in the foreground. (Cal Poly, San Luis Obispo)

La Cuesta Encantada's three guest houses were much in use by Hearst's growing number of visitors. For much of his life, and especially since construction began in 1920, he had been accumulating a wide variety of antiques that were being integrated into the buildings and gardens. Julia Morgan noted that *Casa del Sol* (in this photograph) demonstrated a *"natural habit of attracting the most interesting to herself."* Among Hearst's many auction purchases were components used by his artisans to create these Moorish balcony screens, which he originally called "Harem Bays." (History Center of San Luis Obispo)

The ocean-facing fountain on *Casa del Sol's* West Terrace is one of the most decorative on the hilltop. Its inspiration came from a similar one found in Austin Whittlesey's book of 1917 on Spanish architecture, *The Minor Ecclesiastical, Domestic Garden Architecture of Southern Spain.* Hearst crowned it with a bronze copy of Italian Renaissance sculptor Donatello's *David.* The hilltop workers were adept at integrating, or sometimes replicating, the variety of antique elements that were being used. (Courtesy of Larry Crawford)

Julia Morgan made frequent use of several Old World craftsmen who had their own workshops in San Francisco. Among them was S. Miletin, a specialist in carved stone. In the early 1920s he sculpted these four lions for *Casa del Sol's* "David Fountain" (seen in the upper photo). Miletin modeled them, with slight variations, after the centuries-old originals used in the Byzanto-Gothic fountain that faces the house's courtyard. (Cal Poly, San Luis Obispo; color photo by the author)

49

Hollywood is a huge part of the Hearst Castle mystique. William Randolph Hearst's newspapers and magazines helped create many of the world's first celebrities. His filmmaking company, Cosmopolitan Productions, partnered with Metro-Goldwyn-Mayer (MGM) to make numerous films during the 1920s and 1930s, creating a close association that brought many movie industry personalities to *La Cuesta Encantada*. Norma Talmadge, one of the most popular actresses of the silent-film era, reaches across the sculpture of *Europa* to clasp hands with motion picture mogul Nicholas Schenck. (Bison Archives)

Millicent Hearst posing on the Esplanade opposite *Casa Del Monte*. For the first half-dozen years of construction, she played an active role in the building of Hearst Castle. William Randolph Hearst's respect for his wife's input peppers his letters to Julia Morgan, as seen in this 1925 example: *"Mrs. Hearst doesn't want the chimes. Says they look too [much] like a church so please don't order."* In another letter he discusses her request to remove a portion of a garden wall in the Neptune Pool area: *"Doubtless she is right— she is a pretty good judge of such matters."* However, by late 1925 their marriage was deeply divided by Mr. Hearst's involvement with someone who would play an even greater role in the history of Hearst Castle: Hollywood silent film actress Marion Davies. (California Views)

HEARST CASTLE'S NEW ERA
— 1926-1930 —

Prior to 1926 both William Randolph Hearst and his wife were involved in the decision-making process of Hearst Castle's construction. However, for several years their marriage had been heading toward a separation. "W.R." was in a prolonged and serious relationship with Hollywood film actress Marion Davies, and they had become very close companions. He was also spending more time in California than New York, while Mrs. Hearst looked upon *La Cuesta Encantada* as only a vacation retreat. Although they never divorced, and remained quite friendly toward each other, she bowed out of most of the future events at Hearst Castle and only visited occasionally. For more than 20 years, Marion would fulfill the role of hostess; bringing a vitality and humor that was greatly enhanced by her eclectic circle of friends from the acting community. This large and energetic crowd would bring much gaiety to the hilltop events in the years ahead.

Thus, 1926 began with many changes at Hearst Castle. Previously, its primary purpose was as a family vacation estate. That phase was now ending and a new one had begun: *La Cuesta Encantada* would serve a dual role as the main headquarters for Mr. Hearst's business empire and as an entertainment resort for his increasing number of guests. It soon became clear that additional amenities were needed, and for much of the next 10 years Julia Morgan and the hilltop work crews were kept busy on a seemingly endless stream of new construction projects.

The second floor and mezzanine levels of *Casa Grande* contain a variety of bedroom suites and a large library stocked with anti-quarian books. Above the library were the private quarters for Hearst and Marion Davies, named the Gothic Suite, which they began to use in the summer of 1927. They had separate bedrooms midway up each bell tower, with a sitting room and balcony that overlook the central plaza and distant ocean. Although completion of the elaborate wood ceilings and other interior furnishings would take several more years, the room sizes are quite modest in comparison to the main rooms of *Casa Grande*.

By 1930, two large multi-floor wings had been added to *Casa Grande* to partially enclose the building's rear courtyard. The "South Wing" housed the kitchen and household staff quarters. The main amenity in the "North Wing" was the just-completed movie theater. Many years of work still lay ahead to complete the upper-floor guest bedrooms. Providing the transition of the North Wing to *Casa Grande* is the Billiard Wing, which would eventually be fitted out with a billiard room and additional guest bedrooms. A separate detached building, with two rooftop tennis courts, was being constructed nearby to house the beautiful indoor Roman Pool.

Visitors to the estate were not only from the movie industry. Hearst was very active in world politics and hosted many statesmen, including United States President Calvin Coolidge and Winston Churchill (who became the Prime Minister of Great Britain during the darkest hours of World War II). *Casa Grande's* first-floor Assembly Room was the gathering place for guests to mingle and converse before dinner. All meals were served in the adjoining Refectory dining hall. These two cavernous rooms impressed nearly everyone with the elaborate details of their Renaissance and Gothic features. Antique furnishings included enormous stone fireplaces and colorful tapestries depicting Imperial Rome's defeat of the Carthaginian army of Hannibal.

During these years *La Cuesta Encantada* matured into a hilltop oasis. The Neptune Pool had become a beautifully decorated popular feature, a pergola enclosed a mile-long horseback riding trail, and the hilltop zoo was filled with numerous exotic animals. Surrounding nearly everything were gardens and beautiful countryside. A very exciting and colorful social life filled Hearst Castle with a vitality that was legendary, even as conditions everywhere else were tightening under what would soon become known as the Great Depression.

William Randolph Hearst owned Cosmopolitan Productions, the film-making company that made the movie advertised on this poster: *Beverly of Graustark* (1926). Featured is Marion Davies, who specialized in light comedies and historical-themed movies. She was one of Hollywood's most popular actresses during a career that lasted from 1917 to 1937, appearing in over 50 films and starring alongside Clark Gable and Bing Crosby. She and Hearst first met in late 1915 and soon afterward began a relationship that lasted for more than 35 years. Although Mr. & Mrs. Hearst never divorced, by early 1926 they had begun living largely separate lives. (Author's collection)

MARION DAVIES
In
BEVERLY OF GRAUSTARK
with
ANTONIO MORENO

AGNES CHRISTINE JOHNSTON
from the novel by
GEORGE BARR McCUTCHEON

A Metro-Goldwyn-Mayer PICTURE

Directed by SYDNEY FRANKLIN

Cosmopolitan Production
with CREIGHTON HALE *and* ROY D'ARCY

Marion Davies' first documented visit to *La Cuesta Encantada* was in January 1926, and it soon became a major focal point in her life. Although she had her own home near Hollywood, she and Hearst spent considerable periods of time at "The Ranch." Their domestic partnership ended only when he passed away in 1951. (Author's collection)

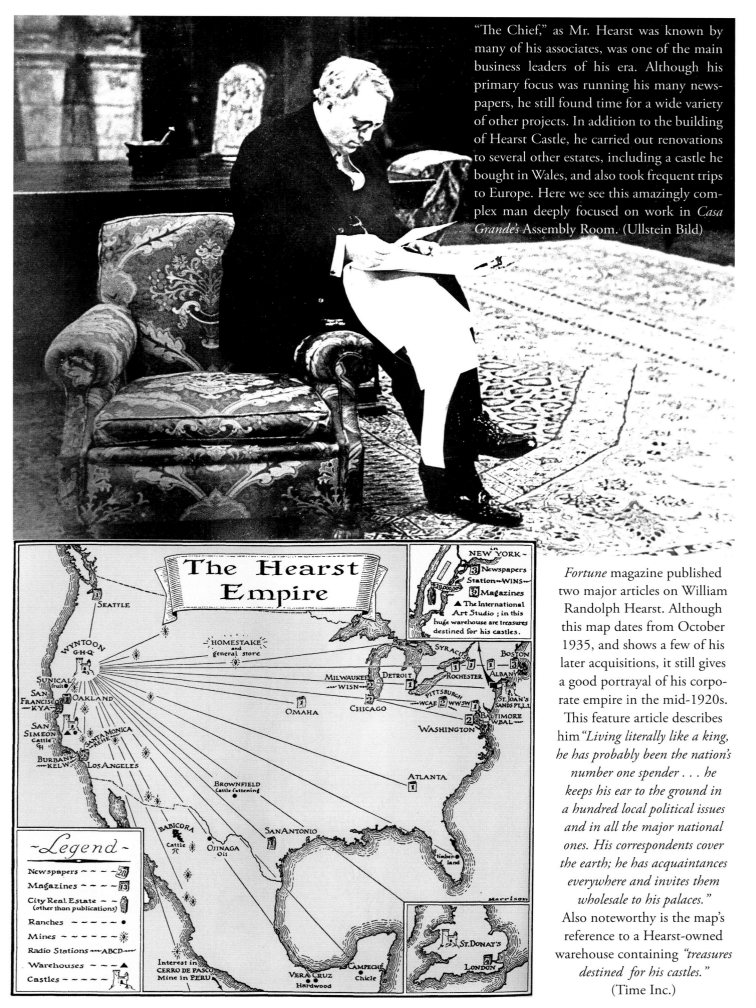

"The Chief," as Mr. Hearst was known by many of his associates, was one of the main business leaders of his era. Although his primary focus was running his many news-papers, he still found time for a wide variety of other projects. In addition to the building of Hearst Castle, he carried out renovations to several other estates, including a castle he bought in Wales, and also took frequent trips to Europe. Here we see this amazingly com-plex man deeply focused on work in *Casa Grande's* Assembly Room. (Ullstein Bild)

Fortune magazine published two major articles on William Randolph Hearst. Although this map dates from October 1935, and shows a few of his later acquisitions, it still gives a good portrayal of his corpo-rate empire in the mid-1920s. This feature article describes him *"Living literally like a king, he has probably been the nation's number one spender . . . he keeps his ear to the ground in a hundred local political issues and in all the major national ones. His correspondents cover the earth; he has acquaintances everywhere and invites them wholesale to his palaces."* Also noteworthy is the map's reference to a Hearst-owned warehouse containing *"treasures destined for his castles."* (Time Inc.)

This view shows how the hilltop looked at the time of Marion Davies' first visit with her Hollywood friends in early 1926. It was taken from atop the hoisting tower that was being used to pour concrete for a major enlargement of the Neptune Pool. Later that year, the remodeling of *Casa Grande's* towers would begin. Plans called for the pointed spires to be replaced by larger versions ornately decorated with cast stone, colorful mosaic tiles, and bronze carillon bells within each tower. Also note the oak tree in its concrete container (on the left) being transplanted to a new location. (History Center of San Luis Obispo)

During the mid-1920s a great deal of finishing work was taking place inside the main rooms of *Casa Grande*. A huge wooden ceiling was being installed in the Refectory dining hall, a lengthy process that meant the adjacent Assembly Room would temporarily fill that role. This rare photograph shows it with the large dining table added for that purpose. The massive 16th-century French fireplace mantel and Flemish-made Scipio tapestries were bought by Hearst specifically to decorate this room. (History Center of San Luis Obispo)

The middle of the three smaller houses, *Casa del Sol,* was given an elaborate courtyard entrance that includes a colorful Qajar Dynasty Persian tile panel and ornately carved marble sarcophagus. An especially interesting feature are the ornamental door grills that were hand-crafted in 1924 by master ironworker Ed Trinkkeller. Blended into his designs are numerous caricature profiles; some are thought to have been inspired by the creations of German author Wilhelm Busch, whose 19th-century illustrated stories are considered to be the precursor to the "comic strip." (History Center of San Luis Obispo)

Equipment in regular use on the hilltop included this steam shovel, here beginning construction of the North Terrace during the summer of 1926. The finished terrace was greatly enlarged from 1929 to 1930, and the huge amount of concrete rivaled that used to make *Casa Grande.* The house in the background is *Casa del Monte.* (Cal Poly, San Luis Obispo)

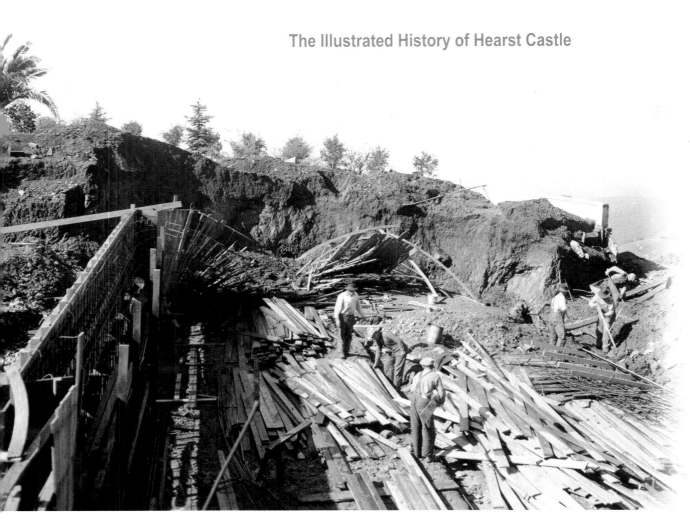

An ever-growing guest list of prominent hilltop visitors was provided with a variety of amenities to enjoy. One of the major projects for 1926 was a substantial enlargement of the Neptune Pool, budgeted to cost $50,000. A huge amount of excavation and retaining wall construction was needed to create a large pool on the uneven slope. (Hearst Castle/ California State Parks)

The concrete work for the Neptune Pool remodel took several months of hand labor. Hundreds of batches were mixed on the lower slope, winched to the top of this hoisting tower and then fed down the sluice to workers with wheelbarrows for distribution into the wood forms. (Hearst Castle/California State Parks)

The enlarged pool was lined with tiles of white Vermont marble and accented with green marble trim. The water was piped in from the reservoir and, depending on the season, heated to between 70 and 80 degrees Fahrenheit. On the far side are various 1st- through 4th-century Roman Empire marble columns and capitals that were purchased by Hearst in 1922 from an antiquities dealer in Rome. They would remain unassembled until their use in the 1934-35 construction of the dramatic Roman temple, built on the same location. (History Center of San Luis Obispo)

The pool's maximum depth is 10 feet (3.5 meters) and the surrounding lighting allowed for nighttime use. William Randolph Hearst was especially pleased when his guests stayed active, and he frequently took the lead in swimming, tennis, and some especially demanding horseback rides into the backcountry. (Ullstein Bild)

Much of the building of Hearst Castle was accomplished by workers such as these, here shown unloading artworks and building materials off a flatbed truck. They labored for long hours under primitive conditions at the remote jobsite, and many of them were expert craftsmen that stayed on the job for years. Their varied skills melded with the vision of the builder, W.R. Hearst, and his architect, Julia Morgan, to create a lasting architectural and artistic achievement. (Time Inc.)

The large number of workers included both permanent and seasonal employees. Most of the construction crew were lodged in the hilltop work camp, the domestic staff in *Casa Grande's* South Wing, and some of those with families resided in the nearby town of Cambria. Hearst also had several private homes built at San Simeon for use by his on-site managers. The two lower photographs were taken in the early 1930s and show a sample of their life: a picnic on the beach and local children putting on a Japanese-themed performance at San Simeon's Pacific School. The small schoolhouse was built in 1881 and is still in existence. (Both photos: Loorz Family Collection)

Casa Grande's original design called for the towers to contain carillon bells, a feature that had been vetoed by Hearst's wife, Millicent, as seeming "too like a church." Following their marital separation, in 1926 the bells were ordered from a foundry in Belgium and the towers remodeled after the *Santa Maria la Mayor* church in Ronda, Spain. The pinnacle-style towers were removed and by the spring of 1927 concrete work on the new towers was completed. This photograph was taken soon afterward, before the addition of colorful mosaic tile and other decorative elements that took well into 1928. The bronze bells were not installed until 1932. (Bancroft Library, University of California, Berkeley)

In 1927, another major enhancement was made to the exterior of *Casa Grande.* Cut slabs of white limestone were added to give the building the appearance that it had been built from large blocks of stone. The effect was so successful that even as work was still underway Julia Morgan was able to predict that the *"stone facing is going to be the making of the building."* (History Center of San Luis Obispo)

The remodeled towers for *Casa Grande* are nearing their final look in this early 1928 photograph, with decorative mosaic tile being added to the new addition. The previous year, Mr. Hearst and Marion Davies had taken up residence in the third-floor Gothic Suite (the balcony leading from their sitting room is seen just below the teak cornice). They each had their own bedroom, midway up the towers; Hearst's was in the south tower, on the right, and Marion's in the north. (History Center of San Luis Obispo)

Adding the finishing details of cast stone and colorful tile continued through the spring and summer of 1928. Upon completion, nearly two years had transpired since the remodeling had begun in 1926. The double-arched windows, seen near the tower tops, would eventually house the carillon bells. Each tower would also contain one of the exotic Celestial bedrooms on the level below (these additions would have to wait until the early 1930s). Hearst's vast land holdings eventually exceeded 250,000 acres, an area that easily encompassed the distant mountains of the Santa Lucia Range. (History Center of San Luis Obispo)

By the late 1920s *Casa Grande* was complete enough for it to be used as Hearst's primary home and business headquarters. The Assembly Room served as his living room and where guests would socialize prior to dinner. Conversations frequently centered on the room's artwork, and "W.R." particularly enjoyed describing the enormous Flemish tapestries that depict Rome's 3rd-century BC victory over Carthage in the Punic Wars. (Loorz Family Collection)

The original caption of this photograph reads: *"Guests playing Bridge in the Assembly Room."* Marion Davies later recalled this room was where guests would flirt with each other while piecing together jigsaw puzzles. The opulent antique furnishing are whimsically offset by the ping-pong table and the RCA Thereminvox sound making device. During this period there was also a pool table (a dedicated billiard room, with two tables, was added to *Casa Grande* in 1933). (Ullstein Bild)

All meals were served in *Casa Grande's* Refectory (the name for a monastery dining hall), the location of many high-spirited evenings of laughter and conversation with Mr. Hearst and his guests. Occasionally, he would even demonstrate his aptitude for yodeling and the latest dance moves! The hanging banners originate from the annual *Palio delle Contrade* held in Siena, Italy, and other highlights include Gothic-style Flemish tapestries showing Biblical scenes from the Old Testament, and a 16th-century ceiling elaborately carved with figures of the Virgin Mary and various saints. (History Center of San Luis Obispo)

William Randolph Hearst was an avid bibliophile and his second-floor library held a wide variety of books from his vast collection. Artwork on display later included these vases dating from Greece's Classical Age. Many of them are among the finest examples found; some are still on display in this room while others now reside in museums. (Hearst Castle/ California State Parks)

The year 1928 included a major expansion to portions of *La Cuesta Encantada's* terraces and Esplanade. This photo, taken from atop *Casa Grande,* shows renovation of the "central plaza," today's Main Terrace. The three guest houses are, from left to right, *Casa del Mar, Casa del Sol* and *Casa del Monte.* (Bancroft Library, University of California, Berkeley)

Enlarging the central plaza's main feature, the lily pond containing the sculpture of *Galatea on a Dolphin*, required moving one of the cherished oak trees. Walter Steilberg, Julia Morgan's structural engineer, explained the process was to *"Design a sort of colossal concrete flower box with holes through the walls so it would drain properly . . . put it on rollers and get enough cables and power up there to move it. I was there when they were just getting it ready to go. The concrete flower pot, you might call it, was at least 15 to 20 feet in diameter, with six-inch thick concrete walls. With carpenter's wages only five dollars a day, it cost $8000 for the one moving."* The cost represented a lot of Hearst daily newspapers, which typically sold for 3 cents each in the 1920s. (Loorz Family Collection)

By the late summer of 1928 the plaza renovation was nearly complete. This photograph shows workers setting brick accents to the paving. The enlarged lily pond featuring *Galatea on a Dolphin* would soon be enhanced with decorative lighting. (Bancroft Library, University of California, Berkeley)

Among the most important of Hearst's employees was Joe Willicombe, who served as his secretary for 30 years. Both men appear immersed in business, seemingly oblivious to the surrounding guests and lion statuary. Many of these conversations would lead to Willicombe sending directives that famously began *"Chief says . . ."* Such instructions could be sent via telephone, teletype or radio. (Ullstein Bild)

The busy summer of 1928 also included renovation of the South Terrace and adjacent Esplanade. This view faces west, looking towards *Casa del Mar*, and was taken just prior to the terrace enlargement. Steps on the right lead to the Esplanade, and the tall plinth that would soon be home to the Egyptian-themed Sekhmet sculptures. (Hearst Castle/California State Parks)

Julia Morgan was a master in landscape design. The expanded South Terrace and Esplanade created much more room to showcase larger art works. This photo shows two Italian Renaissance wellheads, including the famous Verona example, (in the far background, and in color inset) bought by Hearst for his mother, Phoebe, while on a trip to Italy in 1900. With his romanticist nature, he was certainly well aware that Verona was the setting for Shakespeare's *Romeo and Juliet*. (Hearst Castle/California State Parks)

One of the features added to the Esplanade was this fountain, which incorporates original 3,500 year-old sculptures of the Egyptian goddess Sekhmet. The design was created in Julia Morgan's San Francisco office, where she employed several architects and draftsmen. Many of these architectural drawings are the work of her assistant Camille Solon. (Environmental Design Archives, University of California, Berkeley)

The four sculptures used in the Sekhmet fountain were purchased separately by Hearst over the course of several years, between 1924 and 1930, and are the oldest antiques used at Hearst Castle. This late 1920s photograph shows how it looked before it was converted into an Art Deco fountain by marble specialist Lorenzo Cardini in 1933. (Bancroft Library, University of California, Berkeley)

There was a variety of workshops at *La Cuesta Encantada*. Among the busiest was that of two specialists in the art of working with cast stone, Theodore and John Vanderloo. Their tenure began in 1920 with the father, Theodore, and continued throughout the peak periods of construction during the 1930s. Numerous outdoor features, including the lion adornments of *Casa Grande* and the Greco-inspired lighting at the Neptune Pool, are enhanced by their artistry. (Cal Poly, San Luis Obispo)

International guests included Germany's Dr. Erich Salomon, a pioneer in 1920s photojournalism (a field well known to newspaper and magazine publisher Hearst). During his visit, Dr. Salomon took many historic photographs; including this group of hilltop waiters posing with an enormous olive jar in front of *Casa Grande*. It was among several that were later published in a 1931 edition of *Fortune* magazine. The extensive article was about William Randolph Hearst, and was one of the first to present his San Simeon estate to the public eye. (Ullstein Bild)

Swimming in the beautiful Neptune Pool was one of the most popular recreational activities. This is the second of its three versions, each larger and more elaborate. Overlooking the pool are the dressing rooms, with the rooftop Neptune Terrace that offers a panoramic view of the Santa Lucia Range. This building had been completed quickly back in 1928 and did not undergo later modifications — a somewhat unique occurrence for anything built at the Neptune Pool! (Hearst Castle/California State Parks)

As a couple, Hearst and Marion began hosting their Hollywood friends at *La Cuesta Encantada* in January, 1926. An insight into the liveliness of the decade that followed is found in a letter written that summer by Mr. Hearst to Julia Morgan: *"The movie folk were immensely appreciative. They said it was the most wonderful place in the world and the most extravagant dream of a movie picture set fell far short of this reality. They all wanted to make a picture here, but they are NOT going to be allowed to do it."* Morgan enthusiastically responded, *"I liked and enjoyed very much the movie people. They are artists, and alive. It was a pleasure also to see the way those who did not go swimming went around absorbedly taking in the detail."*

Guests from the movie industry would sometimes rehearse upcoming films during their visits. This photograph shows Irving Thalberg (left), the production chief at Metro-Goldwyn-Mayer studio, brainstorming a project at the Neptune Pool with Hollywood executives and actors, including Constance Talmadge (center), one of the major film stars of the era. (Sotheby's)

William Randolph Hearst's driving force ensured the construction process was always evolving. Some of his later additions enhanced the overall architectural theme, while others are controversial for straying from it. Perhaps in the latter category are two wings that were added to *Casa Grande*. Construction of the first, the service wing, was begun in late 1927 and is seen underway on the right side of this photo taken in the fall of 1928. (Some names changed over the years, and this wing is today called the South Wing). The South Wing contains the kitchen facilities and staff housing. (Hearst Castle/California State Parks)

The original caption written on this March 1929 photograph reads: *"Main door to Castle and fish pond"* (only rarely did Hearst refer to his estate as a "castle"). It shows how various elements were skillfully blended into the construction. *Casa Grande's* carved limestone balcony and some exterior ornamentation was specially fabricated during the 1920s. Other features are genuine antique; including the 15th-century Gothic "wild-men" statues that flank the wrought iron 16th-century Spanish door grille. (Hearst Castle/California State Parks)

Posing at *Casa Grande's* front entrance are some of the biggest names of 1920s Hollywood, including Greta Garbo, John Gilbert, Buster Keaton, King Vidor and Irving Thalberg. There were frequently 20 to 50 guests on the hilltop, with higher numbers for the elaborate parties held on special occasions. The crowd was usually a mix of entertainment, business and political celebrities. However, it was Marion Davies' circle of eclectic Hollywood friends that brought the greatest social excitement to those legendary days at *La Cuesta Encantada.* (Bison Archives)

Casa Grande's east courtyard with the South Wing under construction in March 1929. A huge kitchen and pantry occupied most of the ground floor while the upper level was for staff housing. For several years during the late 1920s, a projection screen was set up in this courtyard and movies were shown at night. The small shack, called the Architect's Office, was where Hearst and Morgan spent many hours going over construction plans. It is still there today. (Hearst Castle/California State Parks)

Hearst wanted *Casa Grande's* east entrance and courtyard to be nearly as grand as the main façade. Back in 1925 he had requested Julia Morgan to create an elaborate Venetian theme, including pigeon towers to give his guests an experience similar to *Piazzo San Marco* (Saint Mark's Square) in Venice, Italy. A hilltop zoo employee, Hayes Perkins, described Hearst being photographed in this courtyard *"in the midst of a flock of white fan-tailed pigeons. These, if handled right, swirl down like falling snowflakes."* This 1929 photograph of the elaborate loggia of the Doge's Suite gives a sense of the architectural feeling they were striving for. (Hearst Castle/California State Parks)

The late 1920s was a period of worldwide excitement in aviation. "Hearst's International News Service" sponsored the August 1929 around-the-world flight of this huge German airship, the *Graf Zeppelin*. Guests at Hearst Castle were thrilled when it passed overhead after just completing the first non-stop crossing of the Pacific Ocean. The event was recorded in the log of a taxi driver waiting on the hilltop: *"Graf Zep passed over Ranch at 9:37 pm, flashed hello with search-light. Was answered by flashing of lights on castle towers."* This photograph was taken the following morning at Mines Field, Los Angeles, five days after its departure from Tokyo. (Author's collection)

La Cuesta Encantada shortly before its ten-year anniversary. The caption on this November 1929 photograph reads: *"View of hilltop from Reservoir Hill at peak of activity and construction."* Indeed, the hilltop was a beehive of activity that would not diminish for many more years. (Hearst Castle/California State Parks)

William Randolph Hearst had long wanted to create a legacy for the public to enjoy his vast art collection. His plan was to enclose *Casa Grande's* east courtyard by enclosing it with the proposed Great Hall seen in this Julia Morgan design study. Although it never got off the drawing board, the idea languished in Hearst's mind for many years and he later wrote to Morgan: *"I think this can be made the grandest hall in America . . . when not in use as a ballroom or a banqueting hall, it could be used to contain some of the most important collections . . . we could also use a lot of armor there."* The last is a reference to Hearst's extensive collection of medieval armor. (Hearst Castle/California State Parks)

A second wing for *Casa Grande* was begun in 1929. Its current name is the North Wing, although it was first called the Recreation Wing because of its movie theater and (never completed) three-lane bowling alley. This photo from 1930 shows the construction, and a nice view of the Venetian-themed loggia of the Doge's Suite. The building remains uncompleted, which provides current visitors the opportunity to see how antique elements were used in the making of *Casa Grande.* (Hearst Castle/California State Parks)

Expert craftsmanship is seen throughout Hearst Castle. When installing antique ceilings, workers frequently had to fill gaps with cast plaster that was painted to blend with the original woodwork. In some cases the opposite held true; the room size was changed to fit the art. A caption on a 1930s photograph of this ceiling in the Doge's Suite reads: *"It is a wooden ceiling early 17th century Italian. Art experts agree that this ceiling is composed of three different ceilings."* (Author's photo)

Beginning in the 1910s, movie attendance became a worldwide pastime. During the early years at Hearst Castle, a large outdoor tent was used for showing films. This was followed by the brief use of *Casa Grande's* Morning Room, until the North Wing was added in 1930. A top priority was finishing this movie theater, a scaled down version of the elaborate "movie palaces" built during the 1920s and '30s.

To be invited into Hearst Castle's social scene was much desired among Hollywood's acting community. Seen on the theater's movie screen is Charlie Chaplin, the iconic personality of the silent-film era and forever identified with his character "The Tramp." Both he and Marion Davies were accomplished comedic actors, and their energy greatly added to the liveliness of the hilltop's social events. (Hearst Castle/California State Parks; Chaplin photo, author's collection)

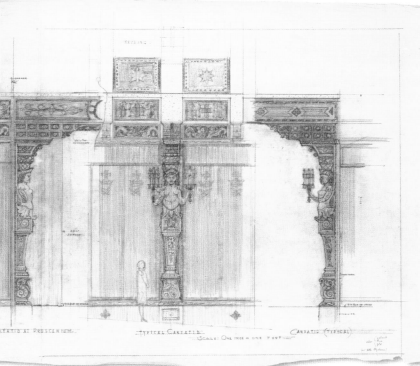

The person illustrated for scale in this construction drawing from Julia Morgan's studio shows the size of the theater's Grecian-inspired caryatid lighting. The produced version differed slightly, and was fabricated in the hilltop's cast-plaster workshop, then gilded and painted. (Hearst Castle/California State Parks)

Marion Davies and Charlie Chaplin pose in the movie theater for the camera of Martin Munkácsi, one of the first fashion photographers. In addition to watching films, many evenings included impromptu performances from the accomplished actors of Hollywood's "Golden Age." Chaplin was remembered for a humorous skit where he mimicked Hearst's enthusiastic descriptions of the artworks that decorated his estate. Miss Davies is holding the telephone that was connected to the projection room. In her lap is her beloved dachshund, Gandhi. (Bison Archives)

La Cuesta Encantada eventually grew to include the world's largest private zoo. Numerous buffalo, antelope, camels and zebra grazed on the lower slopes, while the hilltop area showcased the more exotic animals: lions, chimpanzee, giraffes, tigers, emu, bears and many other species. The caged animals were located close enough to *Casa Grande* for guests to hear the roaring of the big cats, an especially alarming effect for guests arriving at night! (Loorz Family Collection)

Nigel Keep the hilltop's horticulturist for 25 years (1922 to 1947). He was so respected that workers called him "Sir Nigel" and credited him with making a *"fairy land of the place."*

Feeding time was remembered by one of Hearst's guests, Hollywood director King Vidor: *"We'd follow along behind a two-wheeled cart with a man having about a quarter of a cow in there and going to feed the animals, and the lions would roar and get very excited."* The zoo was later expanded with the construction of the "bear grotto" on nearby Orchard Hill. This feature added to the fun of those guests using the nearby pergola horseback riding trail. (History Center of San Luis Obispo)

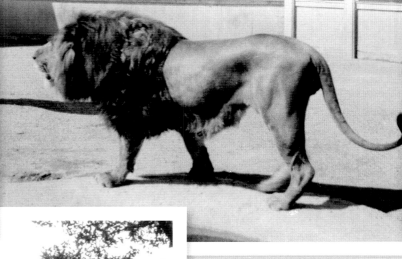

A short distance down the hill from the main buildings were several animal shelters that had been designed in Julia Morgan's studio. Hearst wished to keep many of the free-range animals close to the road so guests could see them. These shelters were built from redwood logs and several are still used by descendants of the original herds. (Taylor Coffman)

William Randolph Hearst and his close friend Francisco "Don Pancho" Estrada on the road leading to *La Cuesta Encantada*. They shared a family connection that began in 1868 when their fathers made a business transaction for some land near San Simeon. Aside from teaching a youthful "Willie" Hearst how to ride horseback, Don Pancho was a true *vaquero* who worked the ranch operations until his passing in 1936. The photo is from the album of Norman Rotanzi, who served as groundskeeper at Hearst Castle for more than 50 years. (Hearst Castle/California State Parks)

Horseback riding was a recreational activity that stretched back to the earliest days of Hearst family camping trips. One of the construction projects begun in the late 1920s was building the Pergola; a covered riding trail that would eventually complete a one-mile loop around nearby Orchard Hill. This photo was taken in 1930, shortly before crossbeams were added to create a shaded arbor woven with climbing flowers and grape vines. Once finished, the pergola was where *"riders could just bend down and pick all kinds of fruit that were blooming. It was one of the most gorgeous things."* (History Center of San Luis Obispo)

Casa Grande's Refectory dining hall decorated for Christmas. Unfortunately, by late 1930 the country was in the grip of the Great Depression and not in such a festive mood. For much of the next 10 years the effects would be felt worldwide with record unemployment and political upheaval. (Hearst Castle/California State Parks)

Hearst newspapers across the country reported the worsening economic conditions. William Randolph Hearst, shown here having dinner in the Refectory, is perhaps reflecting on how to best use his still-ample resources to continue the lavish lifestyle at Hearst Castle. He would be able to do so, at least for a while longer . . . (Bison Archives)

THE GOLDEN AGE AT HEARST CASTLE
— 1931-1936 —

When William Randolph Hearst turned 68 years old on April 29, 1931, he still enjoyed a boundless vitality that allowed him to engage in equal parts work and play. As the world's preeminent newspaper mogul, he had the opportunity to meet some of the most interesting people of his era — many of them would also become his guests at Hearst Castle. Aside from hosting grand parties with Marion Davies, "W.R." still found time to take friends and family on all-expenses-paid European vacation that sometimes lasted for several months. Aside from *La Cuesta Encantada*, he spent considerable time and money overseeing construction projects on three other estates: Wyntoon, a Bavarian-themed forest retreat in northern California; the Beach House, on the shores of the Pacific Ocean in the movie colony of Santa Monica; and St. Donat's, a large estate in Great Britain that featured a medieval castle that had been refurbished to Hearst's eclectic standards.

The 1930s were a period of changing technologies in moviemaking, aviation, and construction. Although the United States was still in the throes of the Great Depression, many people were at work on impressively huge projects such as Boulder Dam, the Empire State Building, and Golden Gate Bridge. There was another that would perhaps have the greatest impact of all: linking the country with an interstate highway system. In the field of the arts, there were new movements such as Art Deco, modern art, jazz and swing music. However, things were not rosy everywhere. Massive worldwide unemployment, and conflicts arising from the Fascist and Communist movements, were beginning to make daily headlines in Hearst's newspapers.

During these years Hearst Castle was in the midst of its Golden Age. It had established a reputation as a social hub for famous personalities that included actors Charlie Chaplin, Cary Grant and Jean Harlow; politicians Winston Churchill and Calvin Coolidge; writers Will Rogers and George Bernard Shaw; and wealthy contemporaries such as Howard Hughes. Frequent costume parties were held on the hilltop and many guests from the film community held impromptu performances inside *Casa Grande's* recently completed theater.

Architecture-as-art was exemplified by the 1932 completion of the indoor Roman Pool. The elaborate mosaic tile-work had taken several years for specialized artisans to design, fabricate and install. During the early planning stages, Hearst had imagined a tropical-themed "South Seas Island on the Hill" oasis that even included a saltwater pool stocked with "a turtle and a couple of sharks." This imaginative idea was soon discarded, but the building that houses the pool was also intended to be furnished with handball and squash courts, and a gymnasium. The outdoor Neptune Pool area also received its share of attention during the mid-1930s with the addition of twin neoclassical pavilions and the Roman temple feature that had been contemplated for a dozen years. By early 1936 this spectacular pool was at last completely finished.

Other major construction during the early 1930s included adding a new upper floor to *Casa Grande*. The main purpose for this project was to build Mr. Hearst's long-awaited Gothic Study, which became his private work space and was beautifully painted with allegorical scenes of life in medieval Europe. The bedrooms for both he and Miss Davies were situated nearby (one in each bell tower) and reached by an elevator. Also completed in the mid-1930s were the uppermost living spaces of *Casa Grande*; the Celestial Suite, with twin bedrooms located just below the tower bells. These fantasy-like bedrooms were reserved for special guests, such as Hollywood actress and newspaper columnist Hedda Hopper, who described them as *"Like a jewel case, with the walls hung in gold brocade. I never knew which meant more to me, the gold room or the view from its windows. When the fog rolled in at dusk from the ocean, the castle floated in its own misty gray sea."*

Even as these building projects were underway, William Randolph Hearst and Julia Morgan continued to plan new ones. For many years, one of their most ambitious ideas was to add an enormous ballroom-museum wing to *Casa Grande,* with the thought that it could eventually become a hall of art open to the public. In a roundabout way, this philanthropic vision for his estate was eventually fulfilled; but it would have to wait for many years. The worsening conditions of the Great Depression were about to catch up with "The Chief" in a way that would unravel all his grandiose plans in the blink of an eye.

William Randolph Hearst using a cowbell to summon his guests, probably for the pre-dinner social hour held in *Casa Grande's* Assembly Room. They could be out playing tennis, swimming, horseback riding or exploring the hilltop gardens and pathways. The May 1931 issue of *Fortune* magazine had a feature article titled *"Hearst at Home,"* which described those days: *"Last year Mr. Hearst spent 204 out of 365 days there. Most of that time he kept his guest rooms fairly full, the court being in session. An average of fifty to sixty guests is composed of senior Hearst executives . . . add to these a stratum of substantial elders and persons of importance . . . with an icing from the cinema world. Finally, season with another celebrity or two."* (Hearst Castle/California State Parks)

This Fokker F-10 "Super Tri-Motor" parked at the Hearst Ranch airport was one of several corporate airplanes used by Hearst in the 1930s. Architect Julia Morgan was now able to occasionally fly down from San Francisco on her weekly inspection trips, and gained first-hand observations of the landing hazards at the primitive airstrip. She made suggestions for later improvements that included a longer runway. (Marjorie Reid Ramsay-Sewell)

Casa Grande was increasingly becoming a corporate headquarters for "The Chief." For several years, there had been plans to add a large office to his Gothic Suite living area. This photograph was taken in the spring of 1931, just before construction began on the "Gothic Study." Creating Mr. Hearst's private sanctuary was a massive job that required removal of the main building's roof and adding a third floor. Many of *La Cuesta Encantada's* features are seen in this view, including the North Terrace (on the left), which is currently used as the receiving area for many of the Hearst Castle tours. (Author's collection)

The hoisting tower, on the left, was used to bring materials up to the third-floor Gothic Study construction. George Loorz, in charge of daily operations, had the unenviable task of coordinating work with the recreational visits of Hearst's many guests. He described the challenge in a 1932 letter to Julia Morgan: *"It certainly handicaps us with the carpentry when we cannot hammer before noon. He has so many guests that any hammering in the forenoon bothers."* The elaborate plan to create a Venetian motif for *Casa Grande's* east-facing courtyard was only partly realized. (Author's collection)

Taken almost exactly one year after the aerial photograph on the previous page, *Casa Grande* shows the newly added third-floor Gothic Study, although several years of interior work still lie ahead. Capping off the roof is the newly poured Celestial Suite's sitting room (the small peaked-roof structure between the bell towers).

The construction camp is at the far right of the photo; at the top are the horse stables, dog kennels and cages for the zoo animals. In the lower left, another phase of remodeling has just begun at the Neptune Pool. This latest project would create an alcove for the large sculpture group: *Birth of Venus*. (Author's collection)

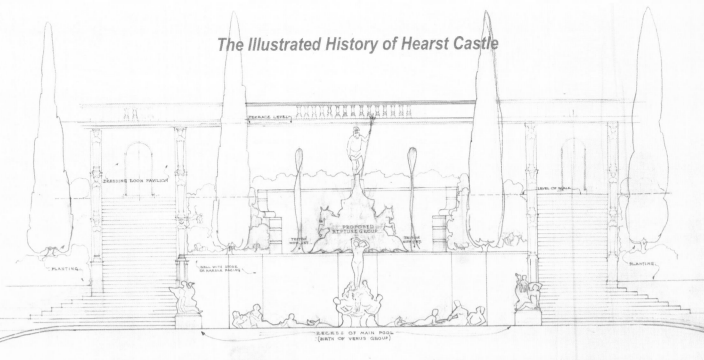

During 1931-1932 the Neptune Pool's "Cascades" feature, for many years the location of the *Neptune and the Nereids* sculpture, underwent a complete transformation. It was rebuilt into a decorative basin featuring the *Birth of Venus* sculpture group seen in the lower portion of this architectural study labeled: *"Scheme for Statuary Grouping at Outdoor Swimming Pool."* The drawing was created in Julia Morgan's San Francisco office. (Hearst Castle/California State Parks)

Also seen in the above drawing is the crowning Art Deco sculpture of the Roman god Neptune rising from the waters in a horse-drawn chariot. Two concept models were created by Parisian sculptor Charles Cassou for Mr. Hearst to select from. He chose this version, with Neptune seated, and the massive marble sculpture would have complimented the Roman temple being planned for the opposite side of the pool (see page 97). Unfortunately, the outbreak of WWII in 1939 prevented its shipment from France. After languishing for many years in storage, the entire grouping was destroyed in a Brooklyn, New York, warehouse fire in 1956. (Hearst Castle/California State Parks)

This construction worker is using a canoe to inspect progress on the pool basin being built for the *Birth of Venus* sculpture group. A dividing cofferdam allowed the main pool to be used during the year-long period of remodeling that included transplanting several fully grown Italian cypress trees. (Loorz family collection)

Venus, and several additional sculptures scheduled for use in the pool remodeling, arrived from France in early 1931. This photograph shows them temporarily staged at the far end of the pool while work was underway on the new basin. (Hearst Castle/California State Parks)

The given French name for Charles Cassou's masterpiece in white marble is *Naissance de Venus,* leading Julia Morgan to playfully refer to this basin as "the ladies pool" shortly before its completion in 1932. Cassou also carved four companion pieces, *Nymphs and Swans,* which were installed around the pool's perimeter. (Doheny Library, University of Southern California)

One of Hearst Castle's most dramatic features is the indoor Roman Pool. The "Gymnasium Building" that houses it, seen in the foreground, was begun in 1927 by excavating below the tennis courts that would also serve as the building's roof. The courts were enclosed by walls during the summer of 1930, and this photo dates from soon afterwards. Behind the arched windows, the process of decorating the pool and interior walls with colorful tile designs has begun, and would continue for two more years. The original hilltop zoo was located just behind where the photographer was standing. (Larry Crawford)

The Roman Pool under construction. During the design phase, Hearst had envisioned building a tropical "South Sea Islands on the Hill" saltwater pool. Julia Morgan carried the idea even further: *"There could be a plate glass partition in the pool and the alligators, sharks, etc. could disport on one side of it and visitors could unsuspectingly dive towards it."* Their plans soon shifted to creating an elaborate Imperial Roman bath, with a décor of deep blue and gold mosaics inspired by those used in the fifth-century mausoleum of Empress Galla Placidia, located in Ravenna, Italy. (Hearst Castle/California State Parks)

On Julia Morgan's staff was Camille Solon, the artist behind the elaborate tile designs of the Roman Pool. Solon supervised a crew of up to 20 specialists that assembled entire sections in San Francisco before transporting them to the hilltop for installation within the Gymnasium Building. The alcove to the main pool is shown as this work was nearing completion in late 1932. It may appear small in the photo, but it is 48 feet long and nearly four feet deep. Salt was initially added to the water to create a healthier swim, but the corrosive effects on plumbing soon put an end to the idea. (Hearst Castle/California State Parks)

Anthony Giarritta (shown here, on the left), along with his brother Joe, were among the specialists who used Solon's templates to hand-set thousands of blue glass and gold-leaf mosaic tiles. The one-inch square Murano tiles were imported from Italy and deliberately set with a slightly uneven surface to give the walls and flooring an ancient look. (Hearst Castle/California State Parks)

The main portion of the Roman Pool is a consistent 10-foot depth, which intimidated some of Hearst's guests. The water was steam heated and the surrounding lamps provide a warm lighting that gives a surreal effect to the cavernous room's decorative tile and neoclassical statues. The romantic environment, and the pool's somewhat remote location, made it ideal for a midnight swim. (Author's contemporary photograph)

As far back as November 1921 Hearst envisioned carillon bells inside *Casa Grande's* towers. For a variety of reasons their installation did not begin until March 1932. This photograph shows specialists from the Belgian foundry engaged in the complicated task of hoisting up the solid brass bells. The man at the top (and shown on the ID card) is Hearst's labor foreman Frank Souza, who worked for 20 years in the building of Hearst Castle.

The 36 chiming bells are played by an electronic keyboard within the North Wing's ground floor. When submitting his original $23,700 price quote to Julia Morgan, the maker of the bells, Marcel Michiels, wrote: *"These bells will be most accurately tuned to give a perfect set of pure, sweet bells as wanted by Mr. Hearst."* Each bell was cast with a different verse, an example reads: *"Tun'd be its metal mouth alone, to things eternal and sublime. And as the swift wing'd hours speed on, may it record the flight of time!"* (Courtesy of Souzan Nelson)

Casa Grande in the spring of 1932, with the carillon bells installation nearly complete. On the roof, work can be seen to add the third-floor Gothic Study and fourth-floor Celestial Sitting Room. The brightly-lit bell towers offered a dramatic sight that could be seen for miles in an otherwise pastoral countryside. (Hearst Castle/California State Parks)

The "Hollywood crowd" were regular guests at Hearst Castle. Much of their journey was via this special train, photographed after its morning arrival in San Luis Obispo (the depot closest to San Simeon). Film director King Vidor was a frequent participant and later recalled: *"We left Union Station in two or three special cars, with a dining car. Drinks and dinner were served on the train and there would be butlers. The name of the train was The Lark. The cars of the Hearst visitors were disconnected in San Luis Obispo and the guests would sleep until the line of automobiles would arrive at 8 a.m. to take them to the Anderson Hotel for breakfast and then continue to the ranch."* (Ullstein Bild)

Extravagant costume parties, usually with a historical or international theme, were frequent occurrences during Hearst Castle's Golden Age. They ranged from spontaneous affairs to elaborate birthday celebrations, such as this "Covered Wagon Party" held on April 29, 1933, to celebrate Hearst's 70th birthday. His son Bill described in his memoirs the *"impromptu speeches and various skits, usually hilarious. The birthday parties called for original costumes, and these created great informality and a lot of humorous make-believe. There was an endless array of food . . . hours of dancing and flirting, all accompanied by a big band playing the latest popular song hits. It all seemed like a spectacular movie scene."* (Bancroft Library, University of California, Berkeley)

Guests at the Covered Wagon Party included this mix of Hollywood notables and Hearst business associates posing in the uncompleted Billiard Room. On the right are Harold Lloyd and his wife, Mildred Davis, both well-known actors from the silent-film era. Lloyd is most remembered for the groundbreaking techniques he used in his movies. The most famous was his daredevil comedic performance in *Safety Last!* released in 1922. Holding the revolver is W.R.'s invaluable secretary, Joe Willicombe. (Bison Archive)

The Billiard Room was completed in the fall of 1933, and was popular with guests awaiting the start of the evening movie in the adjoining theater. This room's elaborate, yet informal, character is due to its smaller size and lower ceiling. In addition to a French Gothic fireplace, the sumptuous surroundings include this 15th-century Spanish ceiling painted with medieval scenes, a Franco-Flemish millefleurs tapestry (named *"Stag Hunt"*) and colorful scenes of Islamic life crafted in 300-year-old Persian tile. (Hearst Castle/California State Parks)

Casa Grande was able to accommodate large numbers of visitors in a wide variety of interesting rooms. This photo shows the Celestial Sitting Room, comprising part of the main building's uppermost floor (the fourth). Its intricate finishing details, and those of the adjoining Celestial bedrooms high in the bell towers, took several years before their final completion in 1934. They have magnificent views of the Pacific Ocean and San Simeon Bay several miles away and 1,600 feet below. (Hearst Castle/California State Parks)

The Celestial bedrooms were very private, exotically deorated, and were usually reserved for Hearst's most-favored guests. Among those visitors was Ludwig Bemelmans, author of the *Madeline* series of children's books, who described the ethereal experience: *"On the wall were curtains twenty feet in length, gold brocade, with draw cords so that you could pull all of them closed and find yourself in an octagonal tent of gold..."* (Hearst Castle/California State Parks)

By the mid-1930s, nearly 15 years had elapsed since construction had begun at *La Cuesta Encantada.* The majestic edifice of *Casa Grande* completed the effect that William Randolph Hearst and Julia Morgan had labored on for so long. Academy Award-winning screenwriter Frances Marion, who wrote scripts for the films of Greta Garbo, Shirley Temple and Mary Pickford reminisced that *Casa Grande* seemed like *"a feudal castle right out of Arabian Nights."* (Bison Archives)

The 1934 completion of *Casa Grande's* upper floor gave Hearst his much-anticipated Gothic Study. Following the evening movie he usually returned here to write articles for, and edit, his many newspapers. Visitors were seldom allowed into this private sanctuary, although on rare occasions it was used for business meetings. Massive plaster-coated steel arches that support the roof are painted with colorful allegorical scenes, reminiscent of a medieval fairy tale. These murals are the work of Camille Salon, the artist who also created the beautiful tile designs for the indoor Roman Pool. (Courtesy of Larry Crawford)

This postcard from the 1930s shows the adjoining Gothic Sitting Room, which was the private living room of Hearst and Davies. Their separate bedrooms were located on either side, accessible by an elevator in the north bell tower. A wide variety of such postcards were available to the public, which indicates the already intense interest in Hearst's *La Cuesta Encantada* estate. (History Center of San Luis Obispo)

Mr. Hearst's bedroom in *Casa Grande's* south bell tower as it looked during his occupancy. In comparison, and perhaps surprisingly, it is rather modest in size and furnishings. One of the highlights is this beautifully painted 14th-century Gothic ceiling that originated from Teruel, Spain.

(Photo courtesy of Hearst Castle/California State Parks)

The religious paintings seen throughout Hearst Castle reflect his preference for this style of Spanish Renaissance art, rather than indicating a particularly devout nature. However, his spiritual side comes through in a stanza from one of his many poems:

"The Song of the River"

So don't ask why we live or die
Or wither or when we go
Or wonder about the mysteries
Which only God may know.

91

Many of the employees that worked at *La Cuesta Encantada*, and on the surrounding ranch, stayed on the job for many years. This photo shows George Loorz, the hilltop construction superintendent from 1932 until 1938, posing at the Esplanade's Sekhmet statue fountain. He was the third of four on-site supervisors during the nearly 30-year period of construction, and worked in close collaboration with Julia Morgan. Mr. Loorz was also involved in the building projects at Hearst's Wyntoon forest estate in northern California. (Loorz Family Collection)

OFFICE OF
WILLIAM RANDOLPH HEARST
LA CUESTA ENCANTADA
SAN SIMEON, CALIFORNIA

Feb. 14, 1934.

Mr. Loorz--2.

The other thing is the stopping of noises in the tower—in fact in both towers. The north tower, however, is much the worse. If I believed in ghosts I would think it was haunted.

Whenever there is any kind of a wind, even a stiff breeze, the moans and groans in the tower are pitiful to hear.

I do not know what the trouble is, although it may be the weather vanes, which are probably old and rusty and creak when the wind moves them.

If it is not that it must be something connected with the bells. If you cannot find what it is any other way, please have someone stay in that north tower bedroom some evening when the wind is blowing, and he will probably be able to determine what the trouble is.

It is a bad trouble, however, and makes sleep almost impossible.

There is a slight moaning in the south tower, but it is only slight in comparison and only noticable when the wind is particularly strong.

It may be due to some similar cause, but it expresses itself in a much less aggravated and aggravating manner.

If we can get these two things fixed up— the fireplace and the ghosts— the house will be much more habitable.

Sincerely,

W R Hearst

William Randolph Hearst was generally a serious perfectionist, which presented many difficulties for his workers. However, he also had a friendly wit as shown in this letter written to George Loorz. The letter was immediately followed up by Loorz's report that the ghosts had been eradicated *"and all is again quiet on the Gothic Front."* The problem was traced to wind whistling through a rooftop ventilation pipe. (History Center of San Luis Obispo)

The Esplanade was surrounded by floral landscaping that connected the three smaller houses to the Main Terrace and *Casa Grande*. Gardeners used flowering plants grown in the hilltop greenhouses or brought in from outside nurseries. On one occasion, Hearst had large areas replanted overnight with white lilies to surprise his guests on Easter morning. Each house had a floral theme and this photograph of *Casa del Monte* shows the climbing bougainvilleas that still brightly decorate its exterior. (Hearst Castle/California State Parks)

The formal garden effect was significantly enhanced by the liberal use of interesting art. This jauntily dressed hilltop guest is leaning against an original Roman marble sarcophagus dating from the 3rd century A.D. (Bison Archives)

Photographs of William Randolph Hearst and Marion Davies posing together are rare. Maurice McClure, one of Hearst's later construction supervisors, summarized how many people remembered Miss Davies: *"She had a heart as big as the all outdoors."* Hollywood director King Vidor perhaps did an equally good job describing Hearst's personality: *"There was something of the mysterious and people were in awe."* (California Views)

Many guests arriving from the large metropolitan areas of Los Angeles and New York City found *La Cuesta Encantada's* rural location its most interesting feature. An early Hearst biographer, Mrs. Fremont Older, described how *"His face lights up with tenderness when a young spotted deer breaks away from her herd, as Bessie does, and at sunset clatters up the tiled terraces of San Simeon."* A similar scene is pictured here on the terrace of *Casa del Mar.* (Hearst Castle/California State Parks)

This photograph of the "Civil War Party" of 1934 was taken in *Casa Grande's* east courtyard. With nearly 100 guests it was one of the largest costume parties held at Hearst Castle. Those glorious days were later described by Marion Davies: *"At the slightest drop of a hat, any occasion at all, we would say "let's make a costume party." Then the telephones would start ringing and we'd get costumes sent up from Los Angeles.* [the location of Western Costume Company, provider to many of Hollywood's movie studios]. *Carloads of people would arrive, and musicians, extra chefs and all that sort of thing. It was really fun."* (Bison Archive)

Playing tennis was a favorite activity on the hilltop ever since the first tennis court was built in 1925. Within two years it was expanded to the two courts seen in this photograph of Hearst and three of his sons, taken on his 71st birthday in 1934. World-class players of the 1920s and 1930s that played here included Bill Tilden, winner of 14 Majors, and Alice Marble, winer of 18 Grand Slams. The tennis courts are located on the roof of the indoor Roman Pool. (Bancroft Library, University of California Berkeley)

Metro-Goldwyn-Mayer studio's Irving Thalberg swings a baseball bat on the plaza in front of *Casa Grande*. Many of Hearst's guests were already familiar with each other, which made for easy and spontaneous camaraderie. Thalberg's film-making talent was so extraordinary that his contemporaries called him "the boy genius." His memory is perpetuated with a special Academy Award named in his honor. (Bison Archives)

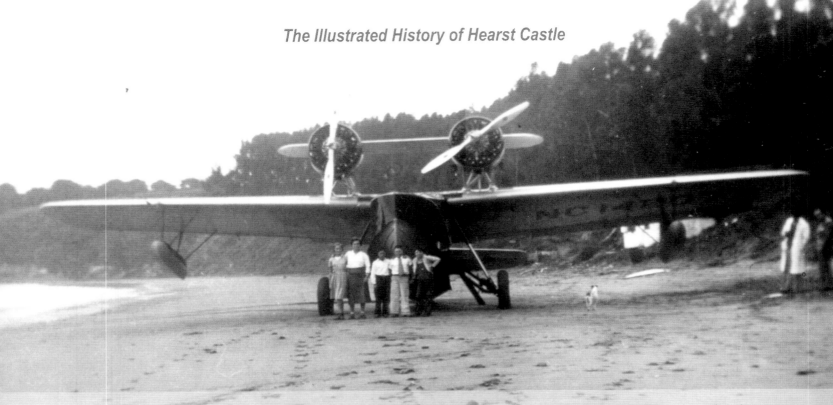

An unusual sight at San Simeon Bay was the arrival of this Douglas Dolphin amphibious aircraft owned by railroad tycoon William K. Vanderbilt II. George Loorz, Hearst's construction superintendent, wrote of the event in a letter dated February 11, 1935: *"Mr. Hearst has a very big party, including some Vanderbilts. They landed in the bay in a very large Amphibian and taxied right up on the sand through quite heavy breakers just as simply as you please."* Mr. Vanderbilt was the great-grandson of Cornelius Vanderbilt, the industrialist who created one of America's wealthiest family dynasties. (Loorz family collection)

From the late 1920s through the post-WWII era, Hearst continually upgraded his fleet of aircraft and enlarged the ranch airport several times. During the summer of 1935, he purchased two Stinson tri-motor airplanes and built this hanger. One of the pilots during this period was Ray Crawford, believed to be the man on the left, with one of the new Stinsons. (Marjorie Reid Ramsay-Sewell)

The largest construction project during 1934 and 1935 was the final remodeling of the Neptune Pool. It included a significant expansion in size, with additional Vermont marble tiles added by the same crew that did the original work in 1927. The most dramatic improvement was adding twin neoclassical pavilions and the long-awaited Roman temple. This Julia Morgan letter to George Loorz is typical of the attention to detail that permeates the hundreds that she wrote during the building of Hearst Castle. (History Center of San Luis Obispo)

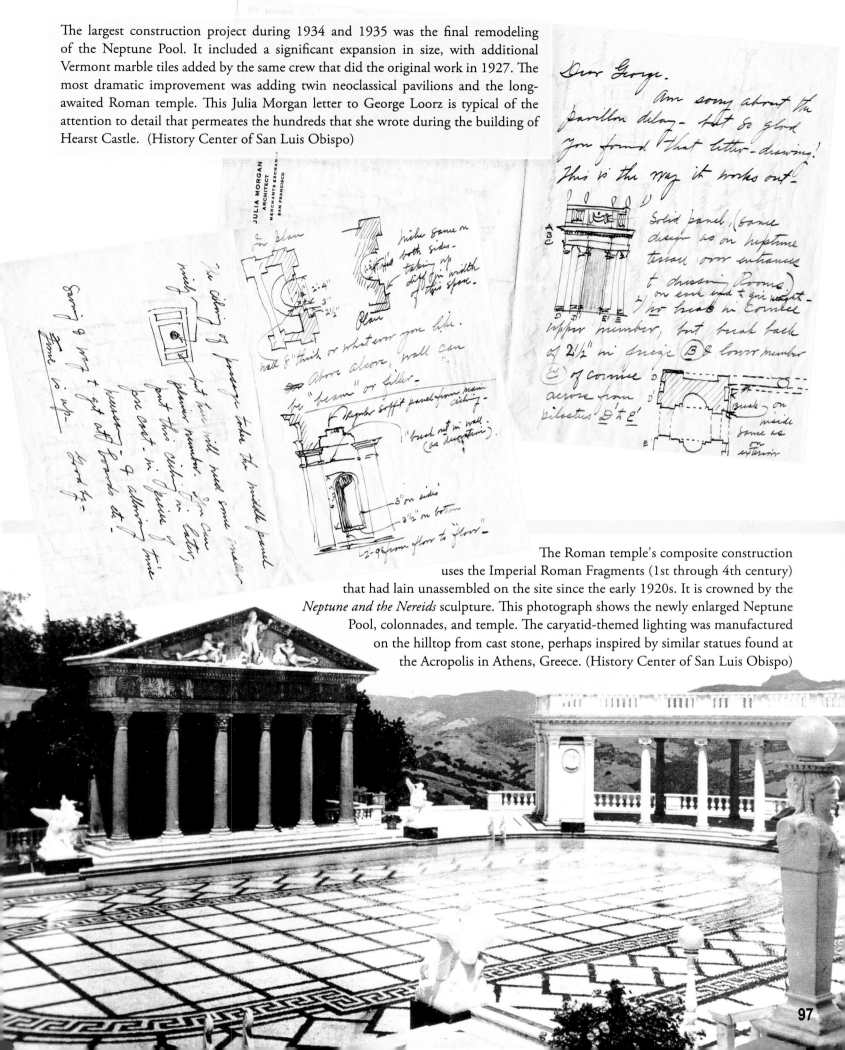

The Roman temple's composite construction uses the Imperial Roman Fragments (1st through 4th century) that had lain unassembled on the site since the early 1920s. It is crowned by the *Neptune and the Nereids* sculpture. This photograph shows the newly enlarged Neptune Pool, colonnades, and temple. The caryatid-themed lighting was manufactured on the hilltop from cast stone, perhaps inspired by similar statues found at the Acropolis in Athens, Greece. (History Center of San Luis Obispo)

Bright sunlight shining through the Refectory's Gothic windows indicates a luncheon is being served. William Randolph Hearst is seated at the center of the table; the pulled-out chair opposite him was usually occupied by Marion Davies. Following, the evening meals, this room was frequently the scene for lively banter, toasts and the occasional speech. Hearst liked the high windows that would allow *"inquisitive little stars at night peeking in to see what all the racket is about."* Seen behind Mr. Hearst is his butler Albert Redelsperger and a small portion of his world-class collection of 18th and 19th-century European silver. (Hearst Castle/California State Parks)

MENU

La Cuesta Encantada, San Simeon, Calif.

Feb, 9, 1936.

DINNER

Green Split Pea Soup

Roast Ranch Squab

Fried Hominy

Baked Potatoes

Cauliflower & Butter

Baked Tomato

Chocolate Ice Cream

Hazelnut Cake

Small Coffee

Breakfast 9:00 to 12:00 A. M.
Luncheon 2:00 P. M.
Dinner 5:30 P. M.

This dinner menu from 1936 shows the typical fare served at Hearst Castle. The main course of "Roast Ranch Squab" was among the many food items raised on the ranch. The second of Hearst's five sons, Bill, described the ranch's self-sustainability in his memoirs: *"I still remember Pop's old poultry ranch and dairy. He raised turkeys, chickens, quail and other game birds for the family and guests. The dairy had prize Jersey cows that supplied milk, butter and cheese to the castle and the families that lived in the village of San Simeon. A large vegetable garden was situated on the horse ranch."* (Author's collection)

FROM DORMANCY TO RESURGENCE
— 1937-1958 —

Throughout the Great Depression, William Randolph Hearst maintained his expensive lifestyle through a complex array of business interests and the sale of stock in Hearst Consolidated Publications. While some of his enterprises were very profitable, this was not always the case within his far-flung media empire. A massive amount of debt was piling up, especially to the Canadian paper mills that supplied the raw material needed to print his daily newspapers. The tipping point was reached in 1937 when Hearst Consolidated missed dividend payments to its shareholders. Corporate bylaws created a Board of Trustees that mandated Hearst to forestall bankruptcy by selling many of his business assets, including hundreds of items from his vast art collection. *La Cuesta Encantada*, and all its treasures, barely survived intact during this period of financial upheaval; however these calamitous events brought a sudden end to the glorious lifestyle and construction projects at Hearst Castle. It would be many years before there would be a return to the energy of those earlier days, and it would prove to be a brief sunset of the era.

Among the many properties owned by Hearst was Wyntoon, a large estate in the forests of northern California. It had originally been developed into a castle-like chateau by his mother in the early 1900s and, following a devastating fire in 1930, had been greatly expanded into an architectural group of fanciful Bavarian-themed houses. The building costs and extravagant furnishings nearly rivaled that of *La Cuesta Encantada*. As the financial woes of 1937 took hold, Wyntoon was where Hearst and Marion Davies began to spend increasing amounts of their time, heralding a transition in their lives towards fewer, and smaller, social gatherings. Although its location was even more remote than San Simeon, there was ample staff and communication facilities that allowed "The Chief" to be fully engaged in the business decisions that would eventually put his finances back in order.

The entry of the United States into the Second World War officially began when Japan attacked Pearl Harbor on December 7, 1941. Over the next few months, California's coastal waters became a war zone after marauding Japanese submarines attacked several ships– including the highly publicized sinking of an oil tanker just outside San Simeon Bay. While these dramatic events unfolded, Hearst and Marion were residing at Wyntoon (and had been since the previous April) and remained there for much of the war. This period also saw a large increase in newspaper sales and advertising revenue, which allowed Hearst to reduce much of his outstanding debt and regain corporate control.

In the summer of 1944 a catastrophic fire at Wyntoon prompted their return to *La Cuesta Encantada* that November. When the war ended in 1945, restrictions on civilian construction were relaxed and new projects could begin. However, Julia Morgan was in somewhat frail health and could only participate as an occasional consultant. A new architect and construction superintendent, both with previous experience on the job, led this final phase of building. The North and South Wings of *Casa Grande* received a major expansion, and the ranch airport was rebuilt to accommodate larger aircraft. The area was once again alive with nearly one hundred workers, with Hearst and Marion living in *Casa del Mar* and occasionally entertaining small numbers of guests amidst the splendor of the earlier days.

However, by early 1947 it was increasingly clear that Hearst was in declining health and needed to be closer to proper medical care. On May 2, several days after his 84th birthday, he bade a tearful goodbye to his beloved ranch and moved into a much smaller estate home in Beverly Hills, near Los Angeles. Building activity at *La Cuesta Encantada* slowed drastically and eventually dwindled to a stop in early 1948. "The Chief" remained keenly involved in business decisions and newspaper editing during the final years of his life until quietly passing away on August 14, 1951.

In 1952 the Hearst family initiated discussions with the State of California towards the goal of gifting *La Cuesta Encantada* to honor the memory of William Randolph Hearst and his mother, Phoebe Apperson Hearst. After several years, the legal process was concluded and public tours began on June 2, 1958. Although he liked to refer to himself as "just a newspaperman at heart," a new era of visitors to Mr. Hearst's hilltop estate would learn that his life story included much more than newspapers.

THE HAND PAINTED PICTURES ON THE WALLS ILLUSTRATE THE FAIRY TALE OF THE THREE BEAR.

THE BEAR FOUNTAIN SCULPTURED BY AN AUSTRIAN LADY

THE BEAR FOUNTAIN — THE BROWN BEAR HOUSE

In addition to *La Cuesta Encantada,* William Randolph Hearst owned several other large estates. This photograph, from the album of his groundskeeper Norman Rotanzi, shows one of the main houses at Wyntoon, located in the forests of northern California. Its development began in the early 1900s when Phoebe Hearst commissioned Bernard Maybeck, one of the most accomplished architects of his era, to design a Germanic "Castle on the Rhine" inspired by her European travels. Following a tragic fire in 1930, it was rebuilt as a cluster of fairytale-themed houses. During the mid-1930s its construction costs rivaled, and sometimes eclipsed, the huge expenditures at San Simeon. (Hearst Castle/California State Parks)

Throughout much of the 1920s and 1930s Hearst spent enormously to support his grandiose lifestyle. Unfortunately, this also sowed the seeds of his financial collapse in 1937. A particularly extravagant purchase was St. Donat's, a 125-room medieval castle in Wales, southwest Great Britain. Alice Head, an employee of Mr. Hearst, acted as go-between during its 1925 purchase and recalled: *"I felt a kind of sinking [sensation] when I realized what we had undertaken."* Although several million dollars were spent on furnishings and renovations, it was used only several times before it was requisitioned by the British military just prior to World War II. Nearly a decade after Hearst's death in 1951, the corporation sold the property, which is now Atlantic College. (Francis Frith Collection)

In 1926 Hearst purchased beach-front property in Santa Monica, not far from Hollywood, and built this Colonial Revival mansion. Ostensibly the residence of Marion Davies, it was named the Beach House and rivaled *La Cuesta Encantada* as an entertainment mecca for their movie-star friends. Several large birthday celebrations were held here for W.R., including the "Circus Party" of 1937 and the "American History Party" of 1938. These became the swan song of the momentous decade of the 1930s when a hundred people, or more, would gather for costumed revelry. Unfortunately, the Beach House was demolished in 1957 and the property redeveloped. It is now a public pool and home of the Annenberg Community Beach House. (Hearst Castle/California State Parks)

On the opposite end of the country was the Long Island, New York, beachfront estate of Millicent Hearst. Bought in 1927, it was originally developed by Mrs. O.H.P. Belmont, the wealthy former wife of industrialist William K. Vanderbilt. Although this photograph from 1931 is captioned *"Residence W.R. Hearst, Beacon Towers,"* it was only used by Mrs. Hearst (their five children were already grown or attending boarding school). The property was sold in 1942 and Beacon Towers was demolished in 1945. (Author's collection)

For much of the 1920s and 1930s, road access linking *La Cuesta Encantada* to the "outside world" came only from the south. Construction of a northern route had begun in 1922, but the progress was extremely slow due to the steep cliffs and geologically unstable terrain. It took 15 years to complete the nearly 100-mile Carmel-to-San Simeon Highway, which remains one of the greatest engineering achievements in California history. (History Center of San Luis Obispo)

Building the road was a dangerous occupation for the workers, many of whom were convicts on work release from the state prisons. Following the highway's official opening on June 27, 1937, its dramatic scenery made it immediately popular with tourists, as George Loorz reported to Julia Morgan from the Hearst Ranch: *"The highway has continued to be patronized at an unusual rate. No one in their wildest dreams had any idea it would be used so much. We are no longer isolated here in San Simeon."* In 1966, the historic road was named California's first official Scenic Highway. (History Center of San Luis Obispo)

Ironically, by 1937 *La Cuesta Encantada* was reaching its full beauty at the same time William Randolph Hearst was facing extraordinary challenges. A massive amount of unpaid corporate debt triggered his business control to pass to a Board of Trustees. In July, it was decided to halt all hilltop construction and lay off most of the workers (although a small amount of work would continue into 1938). This view of *Casa Grande* dates to the onset of those tumultuous years. (Loorz Family Collection)

Despite the gulf that separated them, Mr. and Mrs. Hearst were able to maintain a cordial marriage. This photograph shows them with their five sons and is captioned *"Family reunion at San Simeon 1938."* (From left to right); the twins Randolph and David, George, Millicent, W.R., Bill, and John. It was taken on the Main Terrace, with *Casa Grande* just out of the picture to the right. (Bancroft Library, University of California, Berkeley)

During the 1930s Hearst and Marion Davies suffered the loss of several close friends and family members. A particularly tragic event was the February 24, 1938, crash of one of his Vultee corporate aircraft at the ranch airport. It occurred on a foggy afternoon of limited visibility and killed the pilot, Tex Phillips, and two guests arriving from Great Britain: Lord Terence Plunket and his wife, Dorothe. The accident occurred only a few miles from the hilltop and was clearly heard by Miss Davies, who was severely traumatized by the event. (History Center of San Luis Obispo)

SAN LUIS OBISPO
DAILY TELEGRAM

AN INDEPENDENT NEWSPAPER

SAN LUIS OBISPO (CALIFORNIA)   FRIDAY, FEBRUARY 25, 1938   PRICE 5 CENTS

THE WEATHER
Highest temperature Thursday, 72; lowest, 47. Forecast: North—Fair tonight and Saturday. South—Fair tonight and Saturday; little change in temperature.

PLANE CRASH KILLS THREE

Austrian Nazis Angered

VIENNA, Feb. 25. (UP)—Austrian Nazis demonstrated angrily today in reaction to Chancellor Kurt Schuschnigg's vigorous speech proclaiming Austria's independence and warning against the spread of Nazism in Austria.

The ministry of education ordered the University Technical College at Graz closed because students joined in the Nazi demonstrations. Between 500 and 600 students of the college at Linz paraded, demanding union with Germany and shouting "Heil Hitler! One nation, one Reich!"

The demonstration came after teachers had explained the significance of the speech, was done at colleges elsewhere in Austria. Nevertheless, the majority of the country hailed Schuschnigg as a national hero.

Nazis, restive, suspicious, resentful and somewhat bewildered, were expected to register this week-end, by means of demonstrations—in defiance of a ban on their own Nazi minister of interior—their protest against the chancellor's vigorous speech to the federal diet and his ringing, defiant, words.

Where Three Met Death at Hearst Ranch

Flaming wreckage of the William Randolph Hearst airplane in which three persons met death and a fourth was seriously injured Thursday at 4 p.m., is shown in the above picture, taken shortly after the plane, piloted by T. J. (Tex) Phillips, crashed in a field south of the ranch airport. Lord and Lady Plunket of England, and Pilot Phillips were killed, and Lawrence, also of England, was severely injured. He is in the Sanitarium Friday afternoon was reported "satisfactory."

Late News Flashes

LOS ANGELES, Feb. 25. (UP)—The county grand business association of offering former horse

One Survives Wreck In Fog At San Simeon

Charred bodies of two titled English guests and an airplane pilot lie in the county morgue today as a man is fighting for his life in the San Luis Sanitarium as the aftermath of a flaming crash in a fog on William Randolph Hearst's San Simeon ranch 40 miles north of San Luis Obispo.

One Killed In Reno Plane Crash

RENO, Nev., Feb. 25. (UP)—One person was killed and four persons were injured, one seriously, when a private cabin plane went into a tailspin during a takeoff from the Reno airport early today and crashed from an altitude of 100 feet.

Robert Hancock, 32, San Francisco, described as one of the oldest private pilots still in active service, was killed instantly. Mrs. Louis Clarke De Ruyter Speckels Clinton, daughter of a New York banker and

The dead:
Baron Terence Conyngham Plunket, 38, sixth baron of Plunket, member of the Irish parliament and close friend of King George of England.
Lady Dorothe Mabel Plunket, 38, daughter of Fanny Ward, the actress, heiress to a $3,000,000 fortune, and a lady-in-waiting to Queen Elizabeth.
Pilot T. J. (Tex) Phillips of San Simeon and Burbank, pilot for Hearst and former motorcycle officer of the Montovia police department.

A third guest, James Lawrence, son of Sir Walter Lawrence, a London contractor, is seriously injured but is expected to recover. Lawrence

1936 – VULTEE V1A SPECIAL

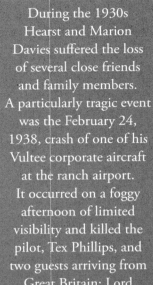

FIFTEEN CENTS   MARCH 13, 1939

TIME

THE WEEKLY NEWSMAGAZINE

HEARST
"At my time of life, you just sit here . . ."
(Press)

Ernest Hamlin Baker

VOLUME XXXIII   (REG. U. S. PAT. OFF.)   NUMBER 11

Losing corporate control to a Board of Trustees came as a terrible blow to "The Chief." However, his son Bill's book *The Hearsts: Father and Son* describes how this event may have been inevitable: *"He understood the financial impact on the company and himself when he continued pouring millions into San Simeon."* That such a legendary man could finally succumb to the effects of the Great Depression was a major news event, as seen in this March 13, 1939, issue of *Time* magazine. (Time Inc.)

Reducing the massive corporate debt required Hearst to sell many of the valuable items gained from a lifetime of collecting. The volume of items included rare books, documents, paintings, furniture and one of the world's largest collections of antique silver. Private sales and public auctions were held to dispose of many items, usually for prices far less than he had paid. This December 1940 photograph shows the owners of Gimbel's department store in New York City previewing items that would soon be offered for sale. Its caption reads: *"A Della Robia statue of Madonna, from the art collection of William Randolph Hearst."* (Library of Congress)

Bill Hearst also recollected his father's despondency over the forced sale of many of his expensive zoo animals: *"He was forced to sell off most of his animals to zoos and other collectors around the country because the company needed cash and lower debts. It really made him heartsick."* These polar bears in *La Cuesta Encantada's* "bear grotto" were likely among those sold to the San Francisco Zoo. For the most part, the herds of grazing herds on the lower slopes were left undisturbed. (Loorz Family Collection)

...we here highly resolve that these dead shall not have died in vain...

REMEMBER DEC. 7th!

World War II had been raging for more than two years before the United States became embroiled following the December 7, 1941, Japanese attack on the naval base at Pearl Harbor, Hawaii. Hearst wrote an editorial from his Wyntoon estate that was published the following day: *Well, fellow Americans, we are in the war and we have got to win it. There may have been some differences of opinion among good Americans about getting into the war, but there is no difference about how we should come out of it.* This poster is one of many that were printed in the successful effort to mobilize public efforts to win the war. (Author's collection)

The war years proved to be a triumph for the manufacturing industry of the United States. One of the most successful innovations was mass-production of "Liberty Ships" for transporting war materials to Europe and the South Pacific. This photo shows the January 1943 launching of the *PHOEBE A. HEARST,* named for William Randolph Hearst's famously patriotic mother. Within four months it was sent to the bottom of the ocean by torpedoes from the Japanese submarine I-19. (Author's collection)

During much of the war, Hearst and Marion Davies lived a life of mostly quiet solitude at Wyntoon. Although the era of hosting legions of visitors for extravagant costume parties was over, Marion later recalled, *"Our happiest times, I think, were at Wyntoon."* On the left is the estate's business hub: the office of W.R.'s secretary Joe Willicombe.
(Hearst Castle/California State Parks)

MR W. R. HEARST and MISS MARION DAVIES

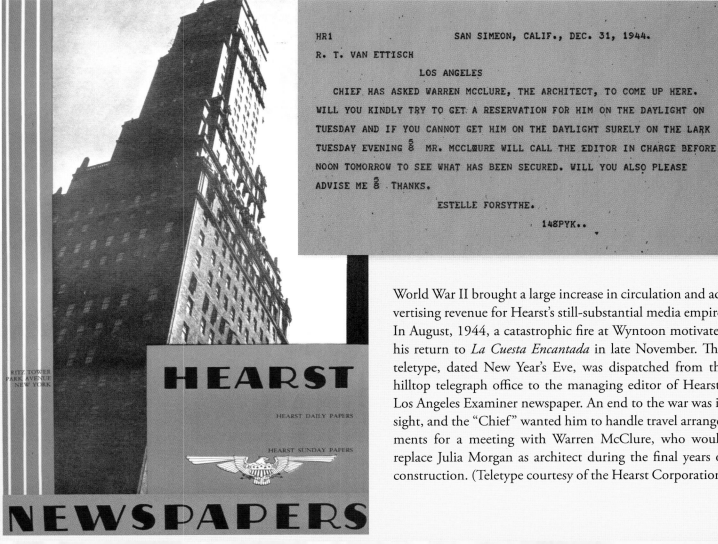

```
HR1                      SAN SIMEON, CALIF., DEC. 31, 1944.
R. T. VAN ETTISCH
          LOS ANGELES
   CHIEF HAS ASKED WARREN MCCLURE, THE ARCHITECT, TO COME UP HERE.
WILL YOU KINDLY TRY TO GET A RESERVATION FOR HIM ON THE DAYLIGHT ON
TUESDAY AND IF YOU CANNOT GET HIM ON THE DAYLIGHT SURELY ON THE LARK
TUESDAY EVENING 5/8  MR. MCCLURE WILL CALL THE EDITOR IN CHARGE BEFORE
NOON TOMORROW TO SEE WHAT HAS BEEN SECURED. WILL YOU ALSO PLEASE
ADVISE ME 2/8. THANKS.
          ESTELLE FORSYTHE.
                    148PYK..
```

World War II brought a large increase in circulation and advertising revenue for Hearst's still-substantial media empire. In August, 1944, a catastrophic fire at Wyntoon motivated his return to *La Cuesta Encantada* in late November. This teletype, dated New Year's Eve, was dispatched from the hilltop telegraph office to the managing editor of Hearst's Los Angeles Examiner newspaper. An end to the war was in sight, and the "Chief" wanted him to handle travel arrangements for a meeting with Warren McClure, who would replace Julia Morgan as architect during the final years of construction. (Teletype courtesy of the Hearst Corporation)

RITZ TOWER
PARK AVENUE
NEW YORK

HEARST

HEARST DAILY PAPERS

HEARST SUNDAY PAPERS

NEWSPAPERS

The increase in profits during the war years enabled the corporate Board of Trustees to pay the creditors, releasing Hearst from the financial shackles that had been in place since 1937. Also, restrictions on civilian construction were lifted after WWII ended in 1945, thus allowing building projects to begin anew at *La Cuesta Encantada*.

New projects included adding a new airport to handle larger aircraft, including this newly purchased Douglas B-23, a converted war-surplus bomber named the "Augusta May" (it was soon replaced by a more suitable passenger model, the DC-3). Seen in this photo are W.R.'s pilot, Allen Russell, and his wife, the plane's namesake. (Courtesy of Wayne Russell)

William Randolph Hearst was a personality on the world stage for much of the 20th century. As with many senior statesmen, his elder years were occasionally taken up with visiting dignitaries honoring his past achievements. In January 1946, leading representatives of the American Legion gathered at *Casa Grande* to present him with the Legion's Distinguished Service Medal. In the center front row is Marion Davies, who had recently celebrated her 49th birthday. W.R. is seen behind her left shoulder. (Hearst Castle/California State Parks)

The hilltop's final era of construction added upper floors to the wing buildings of *Casa Grande* for use as guest quarters. This photograph from early 1946 shows the work underway on the North Wing. A private contractor, Stolte Inc., was hired and described the highlights of working at *La Cuesta Encantada* in its December 1945 company newsletter: *"Every day is finished off by a swim in the magnificent Roman plunge [pool] heated to 80 degrees . . .employees are later invited to attend Mr. Hearst's private theater where a show is given nightly. We've discovered low gear in order to wind our way through the zebras, yaks, oryx, kangaroos, camels, llamas and many other animals that roam freely over the hills."* (Hearst Castle/ California State Parks)

More than 25 years had passed since the beginning of Hearst Castle construction in 1920 and this photograph taken in 1947. *Casa Grande's* east courtyard is dominated by the newly enlarged North Wing, with carved stone windows that continue its Venetian architectural theme. There was little further progress past this point, thus providing today's visitors with an insight into the intricacies that went into the building of Hearst Castle. (Hearst Castle/ California State Parks)

During the period from 1946 to 1947, many of the North Wing's upper-floor rooms were completed. Although Renaissance and Gothic themes were again commonplace, Hearst did furnish other rooms in keeping with contemporary post-WWII styles. Also included in this transition was using forced-air electric heating instead of the problematic fireplaces of the earlier years. (Author's photograph)

Adding new accommodations to *Casa Grande* was scarcely necessary, as Hearst was no longer hosting big events for dozens of guests. The construction continued largely because of his pure enjoyment of the creative process. In this photo, one of the last taken of him on the hilltop, he is shown in the company of his eldest son, George, while holding one of his beloved daschunds. Behind them are *Casa Grande* and the sculpture *Galatea on a Dolphin*. (Bancroft Library, University of California, Berkeley)

This photograph shows the elaborately furnished bedroom in *Casa del Mar* as used by Mr. Hearst in the post-WWII period through May 2, 1947. Advancing heart disease forced him to relocate closer to medical care, so and he and Marion Davies moved to a home they had already purchased in Beverly Hills, California. (Hearst Castle/California State Parks)

THE END OF A FABULOUS NEWSPAPER STORY

William Randolph Hearst died quietly at home in Beverly Hills on August 14, 1951. Throughout his final years he continued to actively direct his far-flung businesses, especially his beloved newspapers. His passing made headlines around the world, where he was widely eulogized for his many accomplishments. *"The End of a Fabulous Newspaper Story"* captions this illustration by cartoonist Cy Hungerford that was published in the *Pittsburgh Post-Gazette*. The "30" pays homage to Hearst's newspaper roots; it was how reporters signed off their stories in the early days of journalism. (Pittsburgh Post-Gazette)

The casket containing Mr. Hearst was flown by private aircraft to San Francisco, the city of his birth. During the journey, the plane overflew majestic *La Cuesta Encantada* and dipped its wings in tribute. The funeral was fittingly held within the Gothic architecture of Grace Episcopal Cathedral on August 17, 1951. Media coverage was extensive and thousands of attendees overflowed onto the street outside. William Randolph Hearst was interred alongside his parents, George and Phoebe, in the family mausoleum at Cypress Lawn Cemetery in nearby Colma. (Bancroft Library, University of California, Berkeley)

Despite the liquidation of much of Mr. Hearst's collections during the 1930s and 1940s, enough remained in his estate to allow donations to public institutions. This 1953 photo shows Millicent Hearst doing the honors at one event. It was published in the *Detroit News* and captioned *"The family of the late William Randolph Hearst presents a 35-piece medieval arms and armor collection to the Detroit Institute of Arts."* The armor is now on display in the museum's main gallery, presenting visitors with the dramatic effect he first achieved at his Clarendon apartment nearly 100 years ago. (Author's collection)

As far back as the 1920s, Hearst expressed the desire for *La Cuesta Encantada* to eventually become a museum open to the public. His son Bill elaborated in the book *The Hearsts: Father and Son*: *"To him, the concept of a museum was an artistic achievement to be shared with others. That is precisely what the great galleries of Europe had taught him. He was saying that we would use the place for a while, temporarily, but one day it would belong to the American people. And he believed in giving them a good show in a breathtaking American setting- an enchanted castle and gardens created in the European grand manner."* LIFE magazine featured "Fabulous San Simeon" in its issue of August 26, 1957. The caption misidentifies the cover photo of the Neptune Pool as the Roman Pool. (Time, Inc.)

By 1957 *La Cuesta Encantada* was in the legal process of becoming today's public attraction of Hearst Castle. William Randolph Hearst's will had first offered it to the University of California, Berkeley, because of family ties dating back to his mother, Phoebe. The university felt it was beyond their scope, and ultimately the 127-acre *La Cuesta Encantada* portion the of Hearst Ranch was deeded to the State of California on January 30, 1958. (Bison Archives)

Much work was needed before Hearst Castle could open to the public. Some of the superfluous sculptures were sold to Forest Lawn Memorial Park, a chain of cemeteries in southern California, which sent a crew to move them to their Hollywood Hills and Glendale facilities. This amusing photo is captioned: *"Entrance to private road at castle."* (Hearst Castle/California State Parks)

"Loading statues with a 10-ton forklift." This sculpture carved by Charles Cassou was one of three used to create the impressive "Diana Group" centerpiece at the main entrance of Forest Lawn's Hollywood Hills location. On the left is Pete Valpiola, Forest Lawn's marble statuary and tile specialist for 37 years. (Hearst Castle/California State Parks)

Five of these trucks were used, each capable of hauling 15 tons. This photograph shows a trailer load of sculptures ready for the journey south. Records show that some individual pieces weighed as much as 10 tons. (Hearst Castle/California State Parks)

HEARST'S ESTATE A CALIFORNIA PARK

Hearst's Beloved Castle Becomes Public Showplace

San Simeon Castle With Its Art Objects to Be Open to Public This Spring

A FAMILY SHOWPLACE

Late Publisher Said to Have Spent $50,000,000 on His 'Enchanted Hill'

By GLADWIN HILL
Special to The New York Times.

SAN SIMEON, Calif., March 2—A lanky young man who has been plodding about a Santa Lucia Mountain ridge in sports clothes changed them this week for a uniform. The switch symbolized the ending of a major chapter in one of the world's most extraordinary stories: the saga of William Randolph Hearst.

The young man was James Whitehead, a Ranger of the California State Park Service, who for some weeks had been technically only the last of myriad guests to experience the imperial splendors of the late publisher's fabulous estate.

Mr. Whitehead's emergence from the legalistic incognito of mufti marked the formal transfer of the Hearst "castle" and environs from a family possession into a public showplace. "La Cuesta Encantada," the enchant-

The elaborate refectory dining room in the castle of William Randolph Hearst's estate at San Simeon, Calif., could seat twenty-four persons at table. The banners are the original flags of ancient Italian nobility. The State of California last week acquired the castle, the outbuildings and 120 acres for conversion into a park, to open in May.

Hearst Castle's opening to public tours was scheduled for the spring of 1958. For several months there had been extensive newspaper coverage, including this article in *The New York Times* that was published in March. (The New York Times Company)

The official dedication and opening ceremony was held on June 2, 1958. Four of William Randolph Hearst's sons were in attendance. His namesake, William Randolph Hearst, Jr., (on the left) assisted California Governor Goodwin Knight in unveiling the commemorative plaque for *"Hearst San Simeon State Historical Monument."* In the far background is the small building where tour tickets first went on sale. (Doheny Library, University of Southern California)

On the day of the dedication ceremony, Governor Knight and his wife, Virginia, received the inaugural guided tour. They were provided with firsthand knowledge of *Casa Grande* by Austine Hearst, the wife of Bill Hearst, who is explaining details of the 15th-century millefleurs Gothic tapestry, *Stag Hunt.* The location is the ground-floor Billiard Room. (Doheny Library, University of Southern California)

Hearst Castle quickly became one of the premier visitor attractions in California. On July 27, 1959, the headline of the *San Luis Obispo County Telegram-Tribune* read: "**Capacity Crowds Touring Castle Daily.**" One of the most popular aspects has always been the ability of the hilltop's guides to interweave their extensive knowledge of *La Cuesta Encantada's* buildings, gardens, and art with the stories of the marvelous personalities who brought it all to life. (History Center of San Luis Obispo)

DIVISION OF BEACHES AND PARKS
HEARST SAN SIMEON
STATE HISTORICAL MONUMENT
ADMIT ONE ADULT $2.00
A370563

LA CUESTA ENCANTADA

PRESENTED TO THE STATE OF CALIFORNIA
IN 1958 BY THE HEARST CORPORATION,
IN MEMORY OF WILLIAM RANDOLPH
HEARST, WHO CREATED THIS ENCHANTED
HILL, AND OF HIS MOTHER, PHOEBE
APPERSON HEARST, WHO INSPIRED IT.

M. GREENBERG'S SONS S.F. CAL.

This bronze dedication plaque is appropriately set into the pavement on the Main Terrace in front of *Casa Grande*. When representatives of the Hearst Corporation offered *La Cuesta Encantada* to the State of California in 1957, their telegram read (in part): *"It is to be a memorial to William Randolph Hearst, who was responsible for its creation and whose hope it was that the State of California receive it in the name of his mother, Phoebe Apperson Hearst. These structures of great beauty with their remarkable collection of works of art and furnishings will be one of California's outstanding attractions and will be a source of pleasure and education to the people of California and the visitors to the great State of California."* (Author's photograph)

La Cuesta Encantada with San Simeon Bay in the distance.
(Doheny Library, University of Southern California)

HEARST SAN SIMEON
STATE HISTORICAL MONUMENT

For much of his life, William Randolph Hearst was a larger-than-life figure. As with many public celebrities, he received extensive media coverage. Several books and magazine articles during the 1930s specifically called attention to his estate homes, especially *La Cuesta Encantada*. At that time, today's Hearst Castle was known equally well for both its exquisite beauty and the famous people that enjoyed it while guests of Mr. Hearst. Also during this period, travelers along the recently completed highway from Carmel to San Simeon (today's Highway 1) were able to catch a glimpse of his home on the distant hilltop. Many of them were aware of the significance of the property, yet no public visitation was allowed.

When William Randolph Hearst died in 1951, his San Simeon ranch passed to his heirs. Although *La Cuesta Encantada* was an asset of the Hearst Corporation it was still very much a family estate. Millicent Hearst survived her husband, and continued to live in her own home in New York, while their sons were now grown and living in scattered locations. The upkeep of *La Cuesta Encantada* was very high and difficult for the family to justify. It was decided to honor William Randolph Hearst and his mother, Phoebe Apperson Hearst, by donating the estate to the State of California (the family would retain ownership of the airport, ranch buildings and agricultural land). Their generous offer was accepted and *La Cuesta Encantada* received another official name: *Hearst San Simeon State Historical Monument*.

The postwar economic boom of the 1950s brought a steady increase in tourism for America's national parks and historical monuments, with California's scenic coastline becoming a premier destination. Also, at this same time, publications were making extensive use of full-color illustrations. The public was able to see the Roman Pool's intricate décor of gold-leaf and blue tiles, close-ups of the carved stone ornamentation of *Casa Grande's* facade, the neoclassical architecture of the Neptune Pool, and the hilltop gardens in full bloom. This media coverage, and the easy access via coastal Highway 1, coincided to make Hearst Castle a large draw for tourism. In June 1958 it was opened to the public, with tours initially offered only from May through October. The experience of walking the same grounds used by a generation of legendary celebrities, against a backdrop of spectacular scenic views, combined to make Hearst Castle an instant success with the public. Over 275,000 people visited during the first year, and year-round tours soon followed.

Hearst Castle exists today because of the inspired collaboration of many talented individuals. Its blend of art, architecture and surrounding natural beauty continues to inspire and delight millions of visitors. Overlooking the Pacific Ocean, the iconic bell towers of *Casa Grande* stand as a magnificent testimonial to the life and times of William Randolph Hearst, Julia Morgan and the skilled artisans who built a castle on an enchanted hilltop.

(Upper photo courtesy of Hearst Castle/California State Parks)

The pastoral setting and architectural theme of *La Cuesta Encantada* brings to mind the environment and history of a southern Mediterranean villa. Adding to this effect are the abundant palm and orange trees that landscape the 127-acre hilltop estate that was built between 1920 and 1947. The wide variety of important artwork seen throughout the estate's gardens, pools and 165 total rooms led to *Hearst San Simeon State Historical Monument* receiving official accreditation as an art museum in 2001.

Hearst Castle's three smaller "guest houses" were constructed during 1920-1924, and each is oriented towards a different scenic view. *Casa del Sol* (House of the Sun, also called "C House") has a west-facing exposure with beautiful sunset views over the Pacific Ocean five miles away. The house's accents of colorful tile, balcony screens and surrounding lion-themed stone sculptures provide a Moorish flavor of North Africa. Its terrace fountain is capped by *David*, a bronze copy of Italian Renaissance sculptor Donatello's depiction of the Biblical story of David's slingshot slaying of Goliath.

The ***David* fountain** overlooks the ocean-facing West Terrace, while on the opposite side of *Casa del Sol* is the Esplanade, with Fritz Behn's white marble sculpture of *Europa* decorating the rose garden.

(Photo courtesy of Hearst Castle/California State Parks)

The largest of the guest houses is *Casa del Mar* (House of the Sea, also called "A House"). It is the most elaborately designed and furnished of the three, and was used by William Randolph Hearst as his personal residence during several years of the mid-1920s and again in the mid-1940s. This is the courtyard entrance just off the Esplanade, with its decorative accents of cast stone, gilded wrought iron and marble busts of the Greek mythological god Hermes (son of Zeus) that are nearly 2,000 years old.

These two interior photos of *Casa del Mar* show the bedroom and bathroom areas used by Mr. Hearst in his last years of living at *La Cuesta Encantada*. His roots on the hilltop began with his childhood days on the family ranch and continued until his final departure in 1947 at the age of 84.

Casa del Mar (on the right) has expansive views of the Pacific Ocean, which provided the inspiration for its "House of the Sea" name. There are two adjoining terraces; seen in the above photo is the expansive **South Terrace** with its two Italian Renaissance wellheads.

The lower terrace is accented by twin water fountains topped by gilt-bronze statues by sculptor Adolf Daumiller; ***The Fairy Princess*** (bottom-left photo) and ***The First Rose***. They were purchased in 1925 from the German artist's studio in Brooklyn, New York. In the far distance is the ranch's private airstrip, still in regular use. The panoramic vistas are the core reason for the existence of *La Cuesta Encantada*, Hearst Castle.

The Esplanade's colorful gardens compliment the climbing bougainvilleas of *Casa del Monte* (House of the Montain, also called "B House"), which was first used by William Randolph Hearst and his wife, Millicent, in 1921. The two marble sculptures, *The Wrestlers* and *Seated Mercury* (shown below), are early 20th-century works by the Romanelli brothers of Florence, Italy.

This Art Deco **Sekhmet fountain** provides the setting for the oldest art objects at Hearst Castle. The four figures depicting this Egyptian goddess were carved from diorite nearly 3,500 years ago. A lioness with the body of a woman, Sekhmet was the powerful protector of the sun god Ra.

Perhaps the most recognized sculpture along the Esplanade is *The Three Graces,* signed "Boyer" and modeled after a famous rendering by 19th-century Italian sculptor Antonio Canova. Aglaea, Euphrosyne and Thalia (Brilliance, Joy and Bloom) are three daughters of Zeus, the most important god in Greek mythology.

During the ten-year period of the mid-1920s to mid-1930s, the **East Courtyard** of *Casa Grande* was where William Randolph Hearst and Marion Davies hosted grand costume parties with up to 100 guests in attendance. On pleasant evenings, motion pictures were sometimes shown on an outdoor projection screen. The Gothic architecture was inspired in part by St. Mark's Square in Venice, Italy.

123

During the 1920s and 1930s *Casa Grande's* **Assembly Room** was the scene of social activities that ranged from card games to ballroom dancing. Europe's Renaissance age is represented in the room's largest decorative features, including the French fireplace mantel, Flemish tapestries and carved walnut ceiling from Italy. The Medieval Age of Christianity is represented by several Italian and Spanish paintings.

(Upper photo courtesy of Hearst Castle/California State Parks)

Italian sculptor Antonio Canova's *Venus Italica* was modeled from the original sculpture (dating from the 3rd century Roman Empire) that France claimed as booty during the Napoleonic Wars of the early 1800s. This example in the Assembly Room was one of several produced by Canova shortly after the original was moved from Florence to Paris.

The circular bas-reliefs represent allegorical renditions of the Greek gods Hercules, Hygeia, Nemesis and Minerva. They were carved in the neoclassical style out of white marble by 19th-century Danish sculptor Bertel Thorvaldsen, who had a studio in Rome.

(Upper photo courtesy of Hearst Castle/California State Parks)

Casa Grande's **Refectory** invites the romanticized imagery of a medieval castle's dining room. The 26-foot-high (eight meter) ceiling is 16th-century Italian, carved with religious images that include St. George slaying a dragon. The table could seat over 40 guests, with surrounding décor of silk *contrade* banners, Flemish tapestries and antique English silver.

A large kitchen and pantry occupy the entire lower floor of the nearby Service Wing.

"The Chief" ran his media empire from the **Gothic Study** on *Casa Grande's* third-floor. While his guests were enjoying the amenities of his estate, he spent long hours in this room editing his newspapers. The ceiling is a skillful blending of 15th-century Spanish with modern load-bearing steel trusses. The arched beams were coated with plaster and painted with scenes of medieval European life by artist Camille Salon in 1934. At the far end of the room is a dramatic portrait of a 29-year-old Hearst, painted by his close friend Orrin Peck.

(Photo courtesy of Hearst Castle/California State Parks)

Casa Grande's east entrance was inspired by the Gothic architecture of Venice, Italy. Sunlight entering through the courtyard-facing loggia illuminates the **Doge's Sitting Room.** This elaborate suite was among the most well-appointed of the guest accommodations and is highlighted by the 17th-century Dutch painting *Annunciation of the Shepherds* built into the ceiling (also, see page 74).

By the early 1930s, *La Cuesta Encantada* had additional amenities that were added to accommodate the steadily increasing numbers of guests. Following the evening meal in the Refectory, the nearby **Billiard Room** was crowded with players and spectators alike while awaiting the start of the evening movie in the adjacent theater. The Franco-Flemish tapestry is named **Stag Hunt.** Mr. Hearst particularly enjoyed his many tapestries from the Medieval Ages, which he described as the "newspapers of their time." He employed several specialists for their repair and conservation.

The North Wing's **movie theater** was built in 1930 and became the scene of many memorable performances by the talented guests of William Randolph Hearst and Marion Davies. This photograph shows the theater's dramatic lighting of cast-plaster statues that are gilded and painted. Similar caryatid figures were first used as decorative ornamentation in the column supports of ancient Grecian temples.

Following the evening festivities, a wide variety of accommodations were available, either within the three guest houses or in one of *Casa Grande's* many bedroom suites. A special privilege was to be staying inside either of the two **Celestial bedrooms** located high in the bell towers. Aside from the romantic effect, guests could enjoy incredibly scenic views from the windows.

(Margaret Herrick Library)

The **Neptune Pool** epitomizes the glory, and difficulties, of construction at Hearst Castle. It began with a modest version in 1924 and underwent two later expansions, each one requiring major engineering into the sloping hillside. The final look was achieved in 1936 with completion of the pavilions and **Roman temple.** French sculptor Charles Cassou's 1930 rendition of *Naissance de Venus,* Birth of Venus, occupies the pool's alcove, with the elaborate Moorish balcony screens of *Casa del Sol* seen on the level above. In 1960 the Neptune Pool was used in the making of the epic historical film *Spartacus.*

Although the **Roman Pool** is an extraordinary decorative feature, its consistent 10-foot depth (over three meters) deterred guests that were less-confident swimmers. During the planning phase, William Randolph Hearst and his architect, Julia Morgan, considered a variety of uses for this building: a gymnasium with indoor racquet courts, multiple baths inspired by those of ancient Rome, even a tropical "salt-water plunge" complete with sharks and rays! Construction began in 1927 and the several-year process of adding the decorative Italian Murano glass tiles took until December 1932. The pool building was excavated and built underneath the hilltop's tennis courts.

(Photo courtesy of Hearst Castle/California State Parks)

Two of Mr. Hearst's favorite recreational pastimes were playing tennis and indulging his love of animals. *La Cuesta Encantada's* first tennis court was built in 1925, and was soon expanded to two courts. During this same period he began purchasing numerous exotic animals to create what eventually became one of the world's largest private zoos. Large concrete pens built for his bears still exist on the hilltop.

The full-circle legacy of Hearst Castle revolves around San Simeon's ranch heritage. While California's coastal development has altered the landscape in many areas, the pastoral countryside of the Central Coast is anchored by the land that encompasses *Hearst San Simeon State Historical Monument* and the current Hearst Ranch. At nearby San Simeon Bay, **Sebastian's Store** and the **Pacific School** predate the construction of *La Cuesta Encantada* and bridge the heritage of yesterday and today.

Sunset at Casa Grande

SOURCE NOTES

Abbreviations Used:

GLP *The George Loorz Papers.* History Center of San Luis Obispo, California.

HSS Hearst San Simeon State Historical Monument, oral history archives.

JMP *Julia Morgan Papers*, Special Collections and Archives, Robert E. Kennedy Library, California Polytechnic University.

INTRODUCTION

vii *"I think California is . . ."* David Nasaw, *The Chief: The Life of William Randolph Hearst*, 214.

CHAPTER ONE: The Origins of Hearst Castle

1 *"We had a glorious . . ."* Nasaw, *The Chief*, 215.

6 *"George Hearst, astute miner . . ."* John F. Dunlap, *The Hearst Saga: The Way it Really Was*, 17.

9 *"to ride after cattle . . ."* Nasaw, *The Chief*, 68.

10 *"A great newspaper is . . ."* Mrs. Fremont Older, *William Randolph Hearst: American*, 559.

CHAPTER TWO: Early Years of Construction: 1919-1922

15 *"The 'Cleone' a very . . ."* JMP, Julia Morgan letter to William Randolph Hearst dated November 21, 1919.

17 *"I get tired of . . ."* Walter T. Steilberg Oral History Project, University of California, Berkeley, 57.

21 *"The men lived in . . ."* Older, *William Randolph Hearst: American*, 532.

23 *"I have sent various . . ."* JMP, Julia Morgan telegram to W.R. Hearst dated April 4, 1920.

23 *"Mr. Hearst and I . . ."* Older, *William Randolph Hearst: American*, 531.

25 *"Mrs. Hearst says the . . ."* JMP, W.R. Hearst letter to Julia Morgan dated September 20, 1922.

27 *"A large man in . . ."* Charles A. Maino, *Old Times*, 24.

CHAPTER THREE: A Castle in the Clouds Emerges: 1923-1925

33 *"It was right out . . ."* Victoria Kastner, *Hearst Castle: The Biography of a Country House*, 129.

36 *"Mr. Rossi is on . . ."* JMP, Julia Morgan letter to W.R. Hearst dated October 30, 1923.

38 *"Yesterday I had a . . ."* JMP, Julia Morgan letter to W.R. Hearst dated November 12, 1923.

41 *"dominant figure of an . . ."* JMP, W.R. Hearst letter to Julia Morgan dated May 1922.

44 *"Sebastian's store was . . ."* HSS, William Nigel Reich oral history, "Memories of my Grandfather Nigel Keep," 14.

46 *"We all called it . . ."* HSS, Adela Rogers St. Johns oral history, "Working with Hearst."

47 *"baronial feast"* Older, *William Randolph Hearst: American*, 539.

49 *"a natural habit of . . ."* Taylor Coffman, *Hearst as Collector: The First Fifty Years, 1873-1923*, 137.

50 *"Mrs. Hearst doesn't want . . ."* JMP, W.R. Hearst letter to Julia Morgan, undated, c. December 1925.

50 *"Doubtless she is right . . ."* JMP, W.R. Hearst letter to Julia Morgan dated September 20, 1922.

CHAPTER FOUR: Hearst Castle's New Era: 1926-1930

53 *"Living literally like a . . ."* *Fortune* magazine, October 1935, 44.

59 *"stone facing is going . . ."* JMP, Julia Morgan letter to W.R. Hearst dated June 8, 1927.

64 *"Design a sort of . . ."* Walter T. Steilberg Oral History Project, University of California, Berkeley, 63.

69 *"The movie folks were . . ."* JMP, W.R. Hearst letter to Julia Morgan, undated, c. June 2, 1926.

69 *"I liked and enjoyed . . ."* JMP, Julia Morgan letter to W.R. Hearst dated June 3, 1926.

72 *"in the midst of . . ."* Taylor Coffman, *Hearst and Marion: The Santa Monica Connection*, 65.

73 *"Graf Zep passed over . . ."* Jane Sarber, *A Cabbie in a Golden Era*, 28.

74 *"I think this can be . . ."* JMP, W.R. Hearst letter to Julia Morgan dated April 26, 1932.

76 *"We'd follow along behind . . ."* HSS, King Vidor oral history, "Work and Play with Hearst and Davies," 9.

77 *"riders could just bend . . ."* HSS, William Nigel Reich oral history, "Memories of my Grandfather Nigel Keep," 29.

CHAPTER FIVE: The Golden Age at Hearst Castle: 1931-1936

79 *"Like a jewel case . . ."* Hedda Hopper, *From Under My Hat*, 161.

80 *"Last year Mr. Hearst . . ."* *Fortune* magazine, May 1931, 67.

81 *"It certainly handicaps us . . ."* GLP, George Loorz to Julia Morgan letter dated August 15, 1932.

83 *"ladies pool"* JMP, Julia Morgan letter to W.R. Hearst dated June 15, 1931.

84 *"There could be a . . ."* JMP, Julia Morgan letter to W.R. Hearst dated May 2, 1927.

86 *"These bells will be . . ."* GLP, Marcel Michiels letter to Julia Morgan dated August 23, 1926.

86 *"Tun'd be its metal . . ."* GLP, Julia Morgan letter to Marcel Michiels dated March 7, 1927.

87 *"We left Union Station . . ."* HSS, King Vidor oral history, "Work and Play with Hearst and Davies."

87 *"impromptu speeches and various . . ."* William Randolph Hearst, Jr., *The Hearsts: Father and Son*, 167.

89 *"on the walls were . . ."* Kastner, *Hearst Castle: The Biography of a Country House*, 151.

90 *"a feudal castle . . ."* HSS, Frances Marion oral history.

91 *"Song of the River"* Older, *William Randolph Hearst: American*, 563.

92 *"and all is again . . ."* GLP, George Loorz letter to W.R. Hearst dated February 22, 1934.

94 *"She had a heart . . ."* HSS, Maurice McClure oral history, "From Laborer to Construction Superintendent," 29.

94 *"his face lights up . . ."* Older, *William Randolph Hearst: American*, 105.

94 *"There was something . . ."* HSS, King Vidor oral history, "Work and Play with Hearst and Davies."

94 *"At the slightest . . ."* Marion Davies, *The Times We Had: Life With William Randolph Hearst*, 215.

96 *"Mr. Hearst has a . . ."* GLP, George Loorz letter to James LeFeaver dated February 11, 1935.

98 *"I still remember Pop's . . ."* Hearst, Jr., *The Hearsts: Father and Son*, 87.

CHAPTER SIX: From Dormancy to Resurgency: 1937-1958

100 *"I felt a kind . . ."* Nasaw, *The Chief*, 349

102 *"The highway has continued . . ."* GLP, George Loorz letter to Julia Morgan dated July 7, 1937.

104 *"He understood the financial . . ."* Hearst, *The Hearsts: Father and Son*, 244-245.

105 *"He was forced to . . ."* ibid, 87.

106 *"Well, fellow Americans . . ."* Edmond D. Coblentz, *William Randolph Hearst: A Portrait in His Own Words*, 229.

107 *"Our happiest times . . ."* Davies, *The Times We Had*, 214.

109 *"Every day is finished . . ."* GLP, Stolte Inc, *Stolte Blueprint* company magazine, December 1945.

112 *"To him, the concept . . ."* Hearst, Jr., *The Hearsts: Father and Son*, 76.

116 *"It is to be . . ."* History Center of San Luis Obispo, Hearst Castle file, Richard E. Berlin telegram to California Governor Goodwin J. Knight dated May 21, 1957.

BIBLIOGRAPHY

Books:

Boutelle, Sara Holmes. *Julia Morgan: Architect*. New York: Abbeville Press, 1988; revised edition, 1995.

Brotherston, Jody G. *Arthur Byne's Diplomatic Legacy*. [Denver, Colorado]: The Lope de Vega Press, 2014.

Chaplin, Charles. *My Autobiography*. New York: Simon and Schuster, 1964.

Coblentz Edmond D., ed. *William Randolph Hearst: A Portrait in His Own Words*. New York: Simon and Schuster, 1952.

Coffman, Taylor. *Building for Hearst and Morgan: Voices from the George Loorz Papers*. Berkeley: Berkeley Hills Books, 2003.

--------. *Hearst and Marion: The Santa Monica Connection*. San Luis Obispo: Publications in Hearst Studies, 2010.

--------. *Hearst and Pearl Harbor: A Memoir in 41 Parts*. San Luis Obispo: Publications in Hearst Studies, 2013.
(The above two books were found online at www.coffmanbooks.com)

--------. *Hearst as Collector: The First Fifty Years, 1873-1923*. Summerland, California: Coastal Heritage Press, 2003.

--------. *Hearst's Dream*. San Luis Obispo: EZ Nature Books, 1989.

Craven, Wayne. *Gilded Mansions: Grand Architecture and High Society*. New York: W. W. Norton & Company, 2008.

Davies, Marion. *The Times We Had: Life with William Randolph Hearst*. Edited by Pamela Pfau & Kenneth S. Marx. Indianapolis and New York: The Bobbs-Merrill Company, 1975.

Dunlap, John F. *The Hearst Saga: The Way It Really Was*. [Medford, Oregon]: Privately Published, 2002.

Guiles, Fred Lawrence. *Marion Davies: A Biography*. New York: McGraw-Hill Book Company, 1972.

Hamilton, Geneva. *Where the Highway Ends*. Cambria, California: Williams Printing Co.,1974.

Head, Alice M. *It Could Never Have Happened*. London and Toronto: William Heineman, 1939.

Hearst, William Randolph, Jr., with Jack Casserly. *The Hearsts: Father and Son*. Niwot, Colorado: Roberts Rinehart Publishers, 1991; revised edition, 2013 (through San Simeon Press, San Francisco).

Hearst, Mrs. William Randolph Hearst, Jr. *The Horses of San Simeon*. San Simeon, California: San Simeon Press, 1985.

Hopper, Hedda. *From Under My Hat*. Garden City, New York: Doubleday and Company, 1952.

Kastner, Victoria. *Hearst Castle: The Biography of a Country House*. New York: Harry N. Abrams, 2000.

--------. *Hearst Ranch: Family, Land, and Legacy*. New York: Harry N. Abrams, 2013.

--------. *Hearst's San Simeon: The Gardens and the Land*. New York: Harry N. Abrams, 2009.

Koszarski, Richard. *Hollywood on the Hudson*. New Brunswick, New Jersey: Rutgers University Press, 2010.

Levkoff, Mary L. *Hearst the Collector*. New York: Harry N. Abrams, 2008

Loe, Nancy E. *Hearst Castle: An Interpretive History of W.R. Hearst's San Simeon Estate*. Bishop, California: Companion Press, 1994

Maino, Charles A. *Old Times*. San Luis Obispo: Jeannette Gould Maino, 1990.

Murray, Ken. *The Golden Days of San Simeon*. Garden City, New York: Doubleday and Company, 1971

Nasaw, David. *The Chief: The Life of William Randolph Hearst*. Boston and New York: Houghton Mifflin Company, 2000.

Older, Mrs. Fremont. *William Randolph Hearst: American*. New York and London: D. Appleton Century Company, 1936

Procter, Ben. *William Randolph Hearst: Final Edition 1911-1951*. New York: Oxford University Press, 2007.

Riess, Suzanne B., ed. *The Julia Morgan Architectural History Project: Volume I; "The Work of Walter Steilberg and Julia Morgan."* Berkeley: University of California, The Bancroft Library, Regional Oral History Office, 1976.

Ryan, Marla Felkins. *Tribes of Native America: Chumash*. New York: Thompson Gale, 2004.

Sarber, Jane, ed. *A Cabbie in a Golden Era: Featuring Cabbie's Original Log of Guests Transported to Hearst Castle*. N.p., n.d. [Paso Robles, California]: Privately Published, 1982.

Soto, Debbie. *Glimpses of a Bygone Era: One-room Schools Along the Hearst Ranch*. San Luis Obispo: Central Coast Press, 2011.

Swanberg, W. A. *Citizen Hearst: A Biography of William Randolph Hearst*. New York: Charles Scribner's Sons, 1961.

Thomas, Evan. *The War Lovers: Roosevelt, Lodge, Hearst, and the Rush to Empire, 1898*. New York: Little, Brown and Company, 2010.

Whyte, Kenneth. *The Uncrowned King: The Sensational Rise of William Randolph Hearst*. Berkeley: Counterpoint, 2009.

Williams, Gregory Paul. *The Story of Hollywood: An Illustrated History*. Los Angeles: BL Press, 2005.

Wilson, Mark Anthony. *Julia Morgan: Architect of Beauty*. Salt Lake City: Gibbs Smith, 2007.

Winslow, Carleton M., Jr., and Nickola L. Frye. *The Enchanted Hill: The Story of Hearst Castle at San Simeon*. Millbrae, California: Celestial Arts, 1980.

Winter, Robert, ed. *Toward a Simpler Way of Life: The Arts & Crafts Architects of California*. Berkeley and Los Angeles: University of California Press, 1997.

Woodbridge, Sally. *Bernard Maybeck: Visionary Architect*. New York: Abbeville Press, 1992.

Magazines and Other Research Articles:

Fortune, May 1931 and October 1935.

Life, August 27, 1951 and August 26, 1957.

Time, March 13, 1939.

McNeill, Karen. "Women Who Build: Julia Morgan & Women's Institutions." *California History*, July 2012.

Pavlik, Robert C. "Crumbling Pergola Testament to Hearst's Grand Vision." *California Landscape Magazine*, April 1989.

--------. "The Design and Construction of La Cuesta Encantada, 1919-1948." Unpublished paper, San Simeon Region, California Department of Parks and Recreation, 1989.

--------. "Phoebe Apperson Hearst and La Cuesta Encantada." Unpublished paper, San Simeon Region, California Department of Parks and Recreation, 1989.

--------. "San Simeon: The Years Without the Chief." Unpublished paper, San Simeon Region, California Department of Parks and Recreation, 1992.

--------. "Something a Little Different: La Cuesta Encantada's Architectural Precedents and Cultural Prototypes." *California History*, Winter 1992/93.

Oral History Transcripts:

Oral History Archives. Hearst San Simeon State Historical Monument.

Walter T. Steilberg Oral History Project. The Bancroft Library, University of California, Berkeley.

Original Source Research:

George Loorz Papers and photograph collections. History Center of San Luis Obispo, California.

Julia Morgan Papers, collection number: MS010. Robert E. Kennedy Library Special Collections, California Polytechnic University, San Luis Obispo, California.

Photograph collections and archives. The Bancroft Library, University of California, Berkeley.